The Video Production Organizer

THE VIDEO PRODUCTION ORGANIZER

A Guide for Businesses, Schools, Government Agencies, and Professional Associations

Aleks Matza

Focal Press

Boston Oxford Melbourne Singapore Toronto Munich New Delhi Tokyo

Focal Press is an imprint of Butterworth-Heinemann
ℛ A member of the Reed Elsevier group

Library of Congress Cataloging-in-Publication Data
Matza, Aleks.
    The video production organizer : a guide for businesses,
    schools, government agencies, and professional associations
    / Aleks Matza.
       p.   cm.
    Includes bibliographical references and index.
    ISBN 0-240-80229-2
      1. Video recordings—Production and direction. 2. Industrial
    television. I. Title.
    PN1992.94.M38   1995
    791.45'0232—dc20   94-44269
                                          CIP

British Library Cataloguing-in-Publication Data
A catalogue record for this book is available from the British Library.

The publisher offers discounts on bulk orders of this book.
For information, please write:

Manager of Special Sales
Butterworth-Heinemann
313 Washington Street
Newton, MA 02158-1626

10 9 8 7 6 5 4 3 2 1

Printed in the United States of America

For Mackenzie

Contents

Preface

If this is your first foray into the world of video production, *The Video Production Organizer* will help you design and produce cost-efficient and effective programs. Even if you already have a few shows to your credit, this guide offers insights and techniques you can apply to your next production.

Your current position may have little, if anything, to do with video. You may be a photographer, copywriter, training specialist, counselor, communications student, or government employee. At the moment, however, you're a producer. Someone in your business or organization has decided to give video a try, and you're in charge.

To what extent you will be involved in the video process depends on many possible factors:

- Your company has a video production department and wants you to assist in a production or to coordinate a project.
- Your organization is considering using video and has assigned you to develop a feasibility study or proposal.
- Your group or agency has produced videos in the past and has asked you to work with others who have already been through the production process.
- You're on your own. You've been assigned to create a video without being offered any assistance or information.

This last point seems far-fetched, but it does happen. I recently heard of a communications employee for a major American corporation who was asked to make a video. She had no idea what she was doing and had no one to turn to for help. She had to learn video production from scratch, and only through sheer determination was she able to complete the task to management's satisfaction. Afterwards, when she was told that I was in the process of writing a book on the subject, her response was, "I could have used something like that. Tell him to write faster next time."

Depending on your own particular circumstances, you may be responsible for making a few phone calls, sitting in on production meetings, or for managing the entire show. You may feel overwhelmed by the responsibility your first time out or you may feel that you're just along for the ride, with only occasional input into the process. With more questions about video production than answers, it's difficult to know where it is you should even begin.

With this in mind, *The Video Production Organizer* was written as a non-technical approach to video production with a special emphasis on managing time, resources, and people. Beginning with a series of basic questions, we will design a program and work with those who will play an important part in its creation. Since your work will be judged by others, you'll also learn how to handle criticisms and objections and how to use evaluations to improve future productions.

WHAT *THE VIDEO PRODUCTION ORGANIZER* WILL DO FOR YOU:

- Help you understand basic video concepts and terms
- Assist you in all phases of video production, from successful planning to the final presentation and program evaluation
- Enable you to locate and use the best services available to make your video stand out from the rest
- Encourage you to get involved in your production at every level
- Instruct you in ways of dealing with company politics and policies
- Show you how to organize your notes and files into a standard production book
- Provide a resource guide of video organizations, publishers, magazines, and directories you can use to increase your knowledge of the business

WHAT DOES IT MEAN TO BE A PRODUCER?

With the exception of commercial television and radio, video is the most effective means of sharing information with a wide variety of audiences. Your programs will influence the way people think and act, whether you're training a handful of employees, sharing prospecting tips with thousands of sales representatives, or presenting a public service message. You're the voice of authority; how you establish that credibility depends on how well you use the medium.

As a producer you'll have to deal with more than just lights, camera, and action. Company politics will determine whether you downplay an issue or play up to special interests. A production house will count on you to deliver reliable and accurate information. Talent must project confidence in a subject as if they work for the company. These are but a few of the day-to-day considerations that will command your attention. The challenge is to move from mystery to mastery as quickly as possible.

Even if your involvement in video production seems limited, understand that you're playing a vital role. There is much to be learned and gained from taking an active part in this unique opportunity. You may not see any immediate benefits, but once you've been a part of any video project, you may find yourself better able to communicate with others, or that the organizational skills you picked up can be applied to your regular job duties. See the experience for what it is, a chance to expand your personal and professional horizons.

WHY A NON-TECHNICAL APPROACH TO VIDEO PRODUCTION?

The video industry has become a technological wonderland over the past ten years, with new software and operating platforms being introduced every day. Editing facilities that once took up whole rooms have been reduced to desktop workstations capable of managing and manipulating images on a scale rivaling the imagination of science fiction writers. Cameras have become lightweight and computerized. Lights are smaller and more powerful. And yet, for all the excitement these innovations have generated, a simple question remains: What good are they without an understanding of the video process itself?

Instead of concentrating on the flurry of changes transforming the industry, *The Video Production Organizer* takes as its inspiration the experiences of two former colleagues from very different backgrounds who found themselves in a very challenging situation.

The first was a sales representative who had been brought in from the East Coast to join the home office training department. Because she had a college degree in communications, it was assumed that she could easily handle her department's desire to produce videos, so she was assigned to work with the company's video division, made up of myself and another producer.

We were all skeptical at first. My partner and I groaned at the thought of working with someone who would probably make unreasonable demands of us, and the sales rep groaned in equal measure at the thought of working with two well-known disciplinary problems who repeatedly violated the company's dress code.

Fortunately, we reached a compromise. Our new producer made it clear that she would give us whatever leeway we needed to get the job done, but at the same time told us that as we worked through our productions, we would

or play up to special interests. A production house will count on you to deliver reliable and accurate information. Talent must project confidence in a subject as if they work for the company. These are but a few of the day-to-day considerations that will command your attention. The challenge is to move from mystery to mastery as quickly as possible.

Even if your involvement in video production seems limited, understand that you're playing a vital role. There is much to be learned and gained from taking an active part in this unique opportunity. You may not see any immediate benefits, but once you've been a part of any video project, you may find yourself better able to communicate with others, or that the organizational skills you picked up can be applied to your regular job duties. See the experience for what it is, a chance to expand your personal and professional horizons.

WHY A NON-TECHNICAL APPROACH TO VIDEO PRODUCTION?

The video industry has become a technological wonderland over the past ten years, with new software and operating platforms being introduced every day. Editing facilities that once took up whole rooms have been reduced to desktop workstations capable of managing and manipulating images on a scale rivaling the imagination of science fiction writers. Cameras have become lightweight and computerized. Lights are smaller and more powerful. And yet, for all the excitement these innovations have generated, a simple question remains: What good are they without an understanding of the video process itself?

Instead of concentrating on the flurry of changes transforming the industry, *The Video Production Organizer* takes as its inspiration the experiences of two former colleagues from very different backgrounds who found themselves in a very challenging situation.

The first was a sales representative who had been brought in from the East Coast to join the home office training department. Because she had a college degree in communications, it was assumed that she could easily handle her department's desire to produce videos, so she was assigned to work with the company's video division, made up of myself and another producer.

We were all skeptical at first. My partner and I groaned at the thought of working with someone who would probably make unreasonable demands of us, and the sales rep groaned in equal measure at the thought of working with two well-known disciplinary problems who repeatedly violated the company's dress code.

Fortunately, we reached a compromise. Our new producer made it clear that she would give us whatever leeway we needed to get the job done, but at the same time told us that as we worked through our productions, we would tell her why we did things the way we did. It was her goal to learn as much as possible about the business in order to fulfill her new job responsibilities, while at the same time keeping us in line (someone had to). She learned well. By the time we had all moved on to other companies, she could not only design effective programs but also learned how to use our camera, editing facility, and other equipment. On a personal level, she quickly became wise to our offbeat ways and knew when we were trying to sneak something past her.

The second was an administrative assistant from the same department as the sales rep. She was a video student at a local college who would often give us a hand on production day and sit in on our editing sessions. While she was very proficient when it came to setting up microphones and lights, she had little concept of the video process as it related to a corporate setting. At school they were assigned a project, instructed how to write scripts, tape scenes, and edit, but there was hardly any attention given to real-life situations, like how to keep a production on time and on budget, or what to do when a manager hands over six videotapes of his daughter's wedding and wants fifty copies by the end of the day. Like the sales rep, she wanted to know as much about why things were done as how they were done.

Because of their willingness to ask questions and to approach video with an open mind, I began to rethink all of the processes and procedures that went into video production, things I had been doing by rote for so many years. Since then I've met and worked with many people in similar situations, professionals from all walks of life who just wanted some straight answers about video. Had they only known about this or that, they could have saved themselves a lot of time, money, and stress. It was a common refrain, one that I kept in mind while writing this book.

I hope you find *The Video Production Organizer* informative, but more than that, I hope it inspires you to develop your own methods. Video is a flexible medium that can be tailored to fit many needs. Take the time to explore the possibilities. Above all, enjoy the show.

Acknowledgments

The author wishes to thank the following people for their help and support: Cathie Rategan of Writer, Inc., for her generosity in providing me with her scriptwriting contract and invoice; Fred Manetti of Fredrick Paul Productions, for his boundless enthusiasm and numerous production stories; PSN Publications for their permission to reprint *The Production Pyramid*; the International Television Association; the Chicago Creative Directory; the State of Illinois Film Office; Richard D. Pope (LGKOV), who covered my back from the rooftops while I walked down the middle of Main Street; and Linda Ramey Matza, for keeping me focused.

STEP 1
Production Planning

Twenty Questions: The Producer's Checklist

So there you are, calmly going about your business, when your boss stops by to give you the news.

"The vice-president thinks that new project we're working on would look great on video. He wants to show it at the next board meeting, and he wants you to put it together. Got time around two o'clock to talk with some people about it?"

By the time any of this sinks in, your boss is gone. Yes, one of the reasons the company hired you was for your communications skills, but video wasn't one of them.

The more you think about it, the more you realize that you can't even program the clock on your VCR. Reading every video production book you can get your hands on would certainly help, but how much of that information will you be able to apply to this assignment? The next board meeting is three months away, but even so that doesn't leave you with a lot of time. Besides, how are you going to put a video together when you're already knee-deep in work?

The most common mistake new producers make when undertaking their first show is getting caught up in the technical aspects of production. They spend too much time reading magazines, catalogs, sales literature, and books trying to figure out what camera they should use or whether quartz or tungsten lights will give them the look they want, and not enough time on basic production planning. That's why there's a video industry. Leave the computer chips and wires in more capable hands. You've got a show to produce.

Before you get ahead of yourself with visions of neglected work and late-night hours poring over lighting handbooks and essays on directing, you need to consider some of the unique characteristics of the business.

WHAT IS CORPORATE VIDEO?

Any program produced for the benefit of company employees, managers, stockholders, clients, prospects, or the general public is considered corporate video.

There are many ways to present information. There's the news pro gram, new product introduction, company history, documentary, new employee orientation, training and executive message, to name a few. Each has its own format and purpose: to inform, instruct, inspire, motivate, and persuade.

"Corporate video" is also a general term. You'll hear and read many names for it, including "industrial video," "non-broadcast video," "business video," "in-house video," and "corporate television."

WHAT DOES A PRODUCER DO?

Video producers perform the same functions as their counterparts in television and film, and that's to assemble, coordinate, and supervise all the elements of production.

On the surface it doesn't look like a glamorous job. The director stands supreme over the cast and crew; actors and actresses play fascinating characters; special effects technicians dream beyond the stars. Meanwhile, the producer sits on the sidelines and watches the action. What fun.

Producing is far from tedious. As a matter of fact, it's the linchpin that holds every show together. The director, crew, and cast cannot function with any sense of harmony without your efforts.

The Video Producer's Role Consists of Four Steps:

Step 1: Production Planning

- Meetings with key project representatives
- Information gathering
- Creation of program treatment and schedule

Step 2: Pre-Production

- Scriptwriting
- Hiring of production company and talent

- Equipment rental
- Arranging program duplication

Step 3: Production

- Studio and location taping

Step 4: Post-Production

- Program editing
- Final viewing and approvals
- Duplication
- Distribution
- Evaluation

HOW MUCH DOES VIDEO COST?

Depending on the length and complexity of the subject matter, you'll spend anywhere between $10,000 and $30,000 to produce a video. Justifying that kind of money requires support from all levels of your organization, not an easy thing to do when budget and personnel cutbacks are the order of the day. Companies often jump into video without considering cost, then abandon the medium when it becomes too difficult to control. Production costs spiral very quickly when left unattended.

Unless you possess an all-around knowledge of production, you're going to hire and purchase outside services and materials.

Guide to Production Costs

Scriptwriter: $200–$350 per page

Director/crew: $1000–$3000 per day

Editing suite: $250–$350 per hour

Talent: $800–$1,000 per person per day

Rentals: $250+ per day or week

Tape stock: $35–$50 per tape

Duplication: $10 per copy

These are merely averages for standard services and are based on a simple shooting schedule along with a need for program distribution. If you add music fees, artwork, and sets, a promotional tape for your upcoming sales contest may end up costing more than the contest itself.

Given inflation and the wide variation in production costs, the quickest way to figure out how much your video will cost is to assume $1,500–$2,000 per finished minute of program. Why such a wide variation in costs?

- Many production companies design packages of services and equipment based on their clients' needs, while others charge flat rates.
- Costs vary from state to state and region to region.
- Equipment quality. Using this year's technology always costs more than using last year's.

HOW LONG DOES IT TAKE TO PRODUCE A VIDEO?

Again, depending on the complexity of your project, it takes a minimum of six to eight weeks to produce a program. We'll set up a production schedule in Chapter 3, but for now divide your program into weekly assignments.

Production Schedule

2–3 weeks information gathering, scripting, and approvals

2–3 weeks production and post-production (editing)

1 week viewing and program changes

1 week duplication and distribution

You can produce a program in less time, but I don't recommend it until you gain enough experience to know where and how to cut corners. Video doesn't lie; if you rush through a production, it will show.

Once you set up a schedule, it's much easier to control the outcome of a program. Deadlines keep everyone on track. Eventually you'll be able to plot the course of a program with very little effort.

HOW DO YOU DETERMINE THE LENGTH OF A VIDEO?

Television and film are organized into neat little segments: TV commercials are fifteen or thirty seconds, news shows and sitcoms are thirty minutes, and dramas are an hour. A standard feature film is two hours long.

Video doesn't play by fixed rules. Theoretically, content should determine program length, but business situations dictate otherwise.

Many of your programs may be watched during conference meetings, some of which last for days. Attendees have to absorb a lot of information in a short period of time and participate in numerous activities. Concentrating on a home office video is not always on the agenda.

Then you have to compete with the environment. Imagine a conference room that's hot and stuffy, with a ventilation system that rattles noisily overhead and acoustics that send every little sound bouncing endlessly off the walls. And just when you think everyone is settled in and ready to give the program full attention, someone turns off the lights. Goodnight, all.

Given these obstacles, your average program should run between five and ten minutes. After that, viewers won't remember much of what you say or do. Here's a guide to help you establish program length.

Video Program Length

New product introduction: 3–6 minutes

Contest promotion: 5 minutes

Motivational message: 5–7 minutes

Executive message: less than 10 minutes

Company information: 10 minutes

News program: 15–20 minutes

Documentary: 20 minutes

News programs and documentaries offer the only exception to the 10-minute boundary. If topics are well written and presented with enthusiasm, the audience members will accept the length as they would any similar type of show they see on TV.

You don't have to stick to these lengths, of course, and there are some shows that can vary depending on the circumstances. If you're producing a program highlighting an upcoming charity drive, for example, your program may be one of several shown at a business luncheon. In that case, your assignment may be to come up with a five-minute overview of what your company is doing to raise money, or fifteen minutes of vignettes showing how employees are doing their part to make the campaign successful.

Training videos were left off the list for a reason. A specific procedure may take ten minutes to explain, while a series of procedures may take up to an hour, with each segment broken up by pauses while an instructor goes over the material with a class. Or you may produce a series of programs lasting several hours spread out over several tapes. In this instance, program time may not be as important a factor as the subject matter.

HOW MUCH TIME WILL VIDEO TAKE AWAY FROM OTHER JOB DUTIES?

Discuss this matter with your manager. Video is very time-consuming, especially if you're doing it for the first time.

Still, you won't be spending every day for the next two months working on it. At first you'll make phone calls as you arrange for and meet with outside services. Then you'll spend time in a studio or on location for taping and editing. Throughout the process you'll conduct meetings with participating departments and the production company to make sure everything is running as it should.

Figure on two to three hours a day to start, whole days toward the end of the schedule when your presence becomes critical to the program's visual look, such as during studio taping and editing. After you've been through a few productions you'll know just how much time is necessary to perform specific tasks. In Chapter 4 we'll look at ways you can best manage your time.

This overview of video production provides a practical framework you can now use when you meet with company representatives to discuss the program.

THE FIRST MEETING

Since the scriptwriter, production company, and talent count on you to understand the subject at hand, you have to become an expert.

This expertise doesn't require a thorough understanding of the thinking that goes into a product or procedure, but it does require a willingness to learn everything you can about it. That's why the first meeting is so crucial. Your job is to assimilate a multitude of facts and design a solid production plan that everyone will work from. Asking the right questions now will point you in the right direction, saving you time and money later.

WHAT TYPE OF PROGRAM IS NEEDED?

When people say they want a video for their new product, what exactly do they need? Do they need to highlight the product, show the product in action, or both? If they want to introduce a new training procedure for billing or customer service, will the training coincide with a new computer software system, or will the video replace or supplement ongoing training classes?

When I worked in a corporate setting, I sat in on many meetings with department managers, trying to get a fix on what type of program they were looking for. Some of the responses I received were very well thought out, with very definite goals in mind. Others were vague and confusing. It was up to me to get them to talk things through, to whittle away the wants from the needs. Not all of these discussions led to actual productions, but it did get them to think about the importance of having a direct application for their video already in mind. The next time we sat down to discuss an idea, they were better prepared and provided a tremendous amount of information for all of us to work from.

HOW SOON IS THE PROGRAM NEEDED?

The board meeting your boss mentioned is three months away, but before then it will be viewed and approved by those involved in the project. Will the vice-president want to show the program to other executives before the board meeting?

Additional presentations will not have a significant impact on your production schedule. Once your program has been edited and approved, scheduling another viewing can be easily arranged. What is important is making sure that if your company doesn't have its own tape player and monitor, one is rented ahead of time.

WHO'S GOING TO WATCH THE PROGRAM?

Always produce one video for one audience. Trying to appease more than one group dilutes program content and power of delivery. One exception is a company history program in which you can address many issues and people.

An educational video showing high school students how to get the most out of their local library requires a basic, hands-on approach, while one covering the latest developments in library science is better suited to a postgraduate audience. Would you stop to explain what a card catalog is to doctoral candidates? Of course not. You'd want to present a working environment familiar to them and get on with the program.

HOW MUCH DOES THE AUDIENCE ALREADY KNOW?

Once you've established who the people in your audience will be, you need to focus on their level of understanding based on the material to be presented.

Members of a hospital trauma unit are familiar with the equipment needed to perform their job, so a training video script should reflect that knowledge with the terms and concepts familiar to them. But if you're teaching people who know nothing about computers how to use one, talking about the intricacies of microprocessors and data retrieval will only serve to further intimidate an already intimidated audience.

Another consideration is to ask what it is your audience really cares about. As a sales person once told me, "Every time we have one of these new product rollouts we have to listen to a bunch of legalese and free market theories. If the company has something to sell, just tell me what it is, how it works, and I'll sell it."

WHAT WILL THE PROGRAM ACCOMPLISH?

List some of the effects the program will have on the audience members. Will it motivate them to sell more, to get more involved in their communities, to make their businesses run more efficiently, or to understand the dangers of environmental pollution? Define these effects in order of their importance.

This information will help the scriptwriter create a program that spends enough time on each of your points to make them resonate and leave a lasting impression. If you've ever watched a political documentary, you know that although its creators may tell you up front what the program is about and what you'll see, they still choose their words and images carefully to make their case. You may not agree with their point of view, but you can't help but listen to their argument. It may even persuade you to think differently.

WHAT MAKES THIS PROGRAM SPECIAL?

Insurance plans are basically the same, and yet benefits, provisions, and riders make certain policies more attractive to consumers. Tool and die companies use the same equipment, but one has a better drafting or computer system. In other words, look for the edge in your subject matter, no matter how small.

"It's just a training video," someone says. That may be true, but behind the instructions and exercises, what is it you're really saying? You're saying that your methods will set the standard for the rest of the industry; that by providing this special training you're helping employees develop a successful career path; and that this expertise will help them adapt to new technologies. These are the things that make your program special.

Think about television commercials you've seen, or those trips you take to the grocery store. Dozens of similar products vie for your attention and dollars every day. What makes one product or service stand out from the rest?

WILL PROGRAM CONTENT CHANGE?
IF SO, WHEN?

This question is very important. If your company is introducing a new group insurance product in June, but in September state laws will change or modify certain provisions of the contract, you'll have to return to an editing suite to change portions of the program that apply to those provisions if you want to keep the program current. This will result in additional production costs and will have to be factored into your budget. You could have the scriptwriter write around the subject, but then the program will lose its focus. Strive for solid presentations.

Of course, there are topics you should avoid. Don't mention product cost or specific people involved in its creation. You never know when prices will go up or someone will leave the company. Never mention dates other than for historical reasons. And stay away from industry buzz-words and trendy phrases. You want the program to have a long and successful shelf life.

WHAT HAVE YOU GOT IN MIND?

You can learn a lot from this question. Someone may have already given the program a lot of thought and mapped out a general outline of the topics to be covered and how they should be presented. If not, a group discussion often reveals highlights and points that need to be addressed. In either case, take detailed notes or make copies of any proposals brought to the meeting. The more ideas you have to work with, the better.

WILL ANYONE FROM THE COMPANY APPEAR IN THE PROGRAM?

Using a business owner, department vice-president, or community leader as a spokesperson adds depth to any message, but these people require special attention. For one thing, any words written for them will have to be approved by them. They won't have much in the way of on-camera or narration skills, either, which means they'll have to spend some time practicing their lines. Passing this information on to a director is vital to allow for extra studio time and coaching.

CAN I COUNT ON OTHER PEOPLE OR DEPARTMENTS TO HELP?

Make sure you can get support if the script requires location shooting in different areas of the company or in another business. The last thing you want is to show up for a taping and have someone say, "No one told me about this." If other people will be involved, write down their names, phone numbers, and what support they'll be providing. Take it upon yourself to contact these people directly to explain what it is you need and how they can help. Don't assume that someone else will do this for you.

ARE THERE POTENTIAL HAZARDS TO CONSIDER?

Do you need to shoot in a chemical plant, factory, or machine shop? A production company will need to know this ahead of time.

The subject of safety is not always on the mind of a producer, but it should be. What's so dangerous about setting up a tripod and camera and shooting thirty seconds of a pipefitter working on a lathe? It's more dangerous than you could possibly imagine. Even if you're shooting a scene in someone's living room, there is always the possibility that something could go wrong.

This is not meant to scare you off shooting in a machine shop or someone's living room, but to make you aware that any video program should take liability into account in the event that property damage or personal injury occurs during the course of a shoot. Despite what you might assume, liability is not solely the responsibility of the production company you hire. A discussion of production insurance will be covered in a later chapter.

HOW MUCH INFORMATION IS AVAILABLE NOW?

Your company wants to present the video three months from now. That leaves plenty of time to put all the necessary information together, right? Not quite.

As an example, let's say you're producing a new product introduction video. During the course of the meeting you're told that the final brochures, flyers, mailers and other sales materials are not back from the printer yet, but that the marketing department expects them within the next few days. The marketing people do, however, have a detailed product description you can use, along with the printer's proofs that show what the pieces will look like. In addition, they tell you what hopes they have for the product and what needs it will fill in the marketplace. No problem. There's enough information available now to get the scriptwriter and production company started and to meet your three-month deadline.

Now let's say that during the course of the meeting you learn that the marketing people have only just begun writing the copy for the sales material, and that it won't get to the printer for another month. They can't promise anything, but maybe they can get a full product description to you within a couple of weeks. That's a problem. You know that the production will take six to eight weeks to complete, which puts your deadline in jeopardy.

There's no easy solution to this problem. Can you still make your deadline? Yes, but it will require an absolute adherence to your production schedule and an understanding on everybody's part that it will be difficult to bring the project in on time if information is continually delayed. If you don't get your information within a couple of weeks, you won't be able to hire a scriptwriter, schedule studio time, or guarantee that copies of the program will be ready for distribution.

No matter what type of program you're producing, you can't do much of anything unless you have information to work with. If you have to research the subject yourself, secure a list of sources to consult and people who can answer any questions.

ARE THERE LEGAL ISSUES TO CONSIDER?

Are there specific subjects you can't mention or scenes you can't show? Do you need to obtain clearance from a state regulatory commission or professional organization?

Let's face it: Coca-Cola is not going to tell you about its secret formula. 3M and Intel are not likely to open the doors to their research and development labs. Companies in the midst of litigation or sensitive financial transactions won't want to talk about it. With industrial espionage a concern in many companies, methods and procedures are closely guarded.

Some companies have a lawyer go over a script before final approval is given. What kind of turnaround time can you expect?

WHO'S IN CHARGE HERE?

Video publications like to talk about picture-perfect productions. The scriptwriter knows the subject matter thoroughly, the crew shows up on time for location taping, the equipment works flawlessly, and management stands by with an encouraging word and an open checkbook.

They never tell you about the times you can't get script approval because the vice-president decided to take the day off, or those days when you have to round up a half-dozen managers to watch a demo reel. In fact, once you get the green light to start a production, key personnel may disappear from the scene. Keep in touch.

Conflicts also arise between departments. A video speaks to the needs of sales representatives, but marketing may have its own idea of how the product should be sold. One vice-president may be at odds with another vice-president. The law department may insist that parts of a contract be included in the script.

Save yourself a few headaches and ask how many people absolutely have to see the script. Who has final approval? Who has final say on the choice of talent and production company?

Use this first meeting to expose and develop as much program content as possible. Follow questions as they lead to other questions. If you don't understand how something works, or who will be responsible for what, say so.

When the meeting ends, the participants will want to see some kind of report or outline they can refer to when discussing the project with others. It also satisfies their need to put everything in writing.

Before you sit down to write your report, you need to supplement your meeting notes with some of the tools of the trade. You need reference materials.

AT THIS STAGE OF THE PRODUCTION PLANNING PROCESS YOU SHOULD

- Familiarize yourself with the basic characteristics of video production.
- Understand the four steps of the production process:
    1. Production planning
    2. Pre-production
    3. Production
    4. Post-production

- Define the needs of your video to help shape program content into a workable production blueprint.

Six Ways to Get the Information You Need

Video professionals enjoy babbling on and on about the complexities of production, what with digital computer animation and video toasters setting new standards of excellence. In many respects they're like scientists—they like to keep the principles of their work shrouded in secrecy, then wow you with the results.

The fact is, producing a video is a lot like building a house. State-of-the-art machinery and space-age materials only impress the naive with money to burn; if the foundation is worthless, so is the house. That's why it's important to prepare yourself ahead of time and take the time to think through and plan a project. There's no reason why your programs can't be effective, provided you have a solid foundation to build on.

So let's start at the beginning. To find your way around the video industry, you have to know where to look. You'll get along much better with reference works, and here's why:

- These materials will give you a consistent source of readily available information. There's not one area of production you won't be able to fathom as long as you have the desire to use it.
- They help establish you as a specialist. The more you know about the people and materials it takes to put a video together, the more your manager and others within the company will come to rely on your abilities, and the better you'll be able to discuss your needs with the production companies and those providing other video-related services.
- A thorough knowledge of the subject will discourage well-meaning peers from giving you a hand in the studio or editing suite.

SIX WAYS TO GET INFORMATION FAST

1. *Find out if your city has a creative directory, "black book," sourcebook, index, or guide to local video personnel and services.*
This is the most important reference book you'll ever have. It lists everything from photographers to writers, production studios and equipment rentals to freelance voice talent.

How can you get one? The easiest way is to call a video studio, ad agency, TV station, photo studio, art supply store, or college communications department and ask what source book the people there use. One of these should put you on the right track.

Here's a sample of a directory's table of contents:

- Computer Graphics; Print Graphics; Presentation Graphics; Video Tape/Film Animation; Service Bureaus; Systems Design/Operation
- Photography Studios; Photographers; Assistants; Stock Photography/Footage; PhotoLabs/Stats; Makeup/Hair; Home Economists/ PhotoStylists/Locations; Sets, Props & Costumes; Stunts, Special Effects; Representatives
- Illustrators; Illustration/Design; Retouching
- Suppliers; Color Separators/Engravers; Color Proofing; Finishers; Printers/Flexographers; Typesetters; Paper Merchants
- Audio Visual Companies; Audio Visual Services; Conventions/ Exhibits
- Production Personnel; Production Studios; Producers; Cinematographers; Directors/Assistant Directors; Writers; Representatives
- Sound and Music Suppliers; Sound & Music Studios; Producers
- Post-Production Services; Post-Production Companies; Laboratories; Distribution
- Equipment Companies; Equipment, Sales, Rental; Grips/Lighting; Studio/Stage Rental; Art & Photo Supplies
- Talent Agencies/Casting; Performing Talent; Freelance Writers; Associations & Organizations
- Advertising Agencies; Business Services; Media Service Organizations; Broadcast; Airlines, Cars & Limos; Hotels/Messenger Services/Restaurants

If you're unable to find a local directory, contact your state film commission to obtain a production guide. Attracting Hollywood dollars is big business these days. Some states have spared no expense to lure major studios with impressive guides touting resident talent. You don't even have to be a tinseltown hotshot to get one. Consult Appendix A for information on your state's film commission.

Don't be concerned that you'll find only film companies listed in a state guide. Video services are also listed, as are a wealth of other services you won't often find in a local creative directory. Another sample table of contents:

- Antique Airplanes, Cars, and Trains
- Boats and Submarines
- Hot Air Balloons
- Medical Personnel and Services
- Museums
- Orchestras and Bands
- Security
- Sports Arenas
- Trailers
- Word Processing
- Zoos

Directories and guides are arranged by subject matter, and in the case of state production guides, by geographical regions. Each section contains short descriptions of company services, clients, and key staff members. Aside from listing addresses and phone numbers, some guides also include fax and telex numbers. Read these books thoroughly! Professionals consider these publications essential to their trade. It's like having a specialized version of the yellow pages at your disposal.

Whatever interests you, remember this: every service listed in a directory wants your business. If you need some advice, or are curious about how something is done, just call. You'll rarely find an unfriendly or uncooperative person on the other end of the line.

Also keep in mind that individuals and companies have demo tapes of their latest work. Ask for one when you call. It's a good way to learn about production.

2. *Purchase or subscribe to video magazines.*
Video publications are written primarily for companies with in-house studios stocked with sophisticated equipment and big budgets, but you can occasionally pick up useful production tips, product and book reviews, and changes within the industry. It never hurts to know who's doing what.

Rates are reasonable, but you can qualify for sample copies and free subscriptions if you meet the publisher's criteria. A library or company resource center may carry back issues. Read them thoroughly before making any decisions. Also check the magazine stand at your local bookstore. Some carry video publications for the home enthusiast that provide step-by-step instructions on a variety of topics.

Many of these magazines contain reader reply cards for ordering information from specific manufacturers. Use these cards to obtain valuable catalogs and other sales material. They'll come in handy later on. Appendix B lists video publications that might be of interest to you.

3. *Join a video organization.*

If you want to know what's going on in your town, joining an organization or attending a meeting has its advantages. An organization can provide valuable contacts, publish membership directories, and attract a wealth of freelance talent. If you know the players, the game is easier to play.

Meetings sometimes highlight a specific product or family of products. They also discuss the business aspects of production or where the industry is going. In all, it's a good way to see how things work firsthand, and by discussing video production with professionals, you can learn a great deal about the business.

There is a down side to joining an organization that you should be aware of. Many are sponsored, run, and attended by companies with large video departments. More than one person has come away frustrated because meetings were cliquish or too technical. Others have found membership fees too expensive to maintain and travel time to meeting sites hardly worth the effort. It's up to you to decide whether a group provides the information and support you need.

Appendix C contains a list of national organizations; call or write for information on local chapters.

4.   *Read books.*

Now that video is available to companies of all sizes and budgets, how-to books have simplified even the most intricate of subjects. Interested in learning how to write scripts on your own, or how to use lighting to give your show a unique look? Need a dictionary to figure out what a gobo is? Look no further; these books will have you thinking and sounding like an expert in no time.

I have listed several publishers in Appendix D to get you started. Again, check with your library or company resource center for copies of books before you order.

5.   *Talk to other companies, especially those in your industry.*

Many people never bother to call other companies to see what kinds of videos they're producing or to ask what resources they're using, and it's a shame because they're missing a wonderful opportunity.

The benefits are well worth the effort. Once you establish a rapport with other producers, it's easy to develop your own network. Instead of consulting books, you can pick up the phone and talk your way through a problem, share a production story, swap tapes, and pass on shortcuts and other time-saving tips.

Many years ago I wrote and produced a history program for a corporation's anniversary celebration. The program was originally produced for employees and stockholders, but six months later I received a long-distance call from a company in Ohio requesting a copy. It seems the vice-president of my company knew the vice-president of the Ohio company and bragged that we had produced an anniversary video. The other vice-president mentioned that his company had an anniversary coming up—could he see how we did it?

There are many factors that will influence the outcome of your videos, just as the finished product will influence others. Nothing in this business is created and used in a vacuum.

6. *Watch television and movies.*
This is one of the few books you'll read in which the author makes a strong case for watching television.

As you gain production experience, you'll also become an astute observer of commercials, television programs, and movies. Why? By watching TV and movies you'll pick up visual details you might not have noticed before. You'll learn the art of continuity, which weaves a visual thread from one scene to another. And you'll appreciate how advertisers manage to fit so much into a 30-second spot.

At this point I have to admit to ruining the viewing pleasures of more than one person, especially when it comes to feature films. While watching a video with friends, I have often announced that I could see a microphone reflected in a window, or point out a prop that mysteriously moved from one end of a desk to another from scene to scene. Before long, I have everyone looking for errors, with the tape running back and forth until everyone can catch them. Television shows rank a close second, with commercials checking in virtually error-free. There's no excuse for my pointing out such errors, but once you've spent an inordinate amount of your life in an editing suite, where every frame and scene is matched to the one before and after, it's hard not to notice when something doesn't look right.

What you learn from watching movies and television can be applied to video. In other words, as you concentrate more and more on the content and look of your programs, you'll become a more active participant instead of simply a viewer.

AT THIS STAGE OF THE PRODUCTION PLANNING PROCESS YOU SHOULD

- Obtain a local creative directory or state film commission production guide (Appendix A).
- Purchase or subscribe to video magazines (Appendix B).
- Join a video organization or attend a meeting (Appendix C).
- Read books on the technical aspects of video production (Appendix D).
- Talk to other companies producing videos.
- Watch movies and television with an eye toward production elements, content, and delivery.

3

How to Write a Treatment and Develop a Production Schedule

Chapters 1 and 2 addressed basic production elements and resources utilized by the video producer. In this chapter, you will analyze your meeting notes and merge them into a program blueprint known as a treatment.

A treatment briefly describes the goals, people, and services involved in a production. If enough information is available, the treatment also includes a synopsis or overview of the material to be covered. After reading a complete treatment, even those unacquainted with your project will understand what the program is all about.

According to many video books and magazines, treatments are prepared by scriptwriters who attend video planning meetings and work closely with managers and executives to craft a brilliant and successful program. This is wishful thinking. Your video needs to be launched as soon as possible; you may not have time to wait for a scriptwriter to do the job, in which case you're better off developing the treatment yourself.

This is not to say that you should never let scriptwriters help you develop a program treatment. Depending on how soon the video is needed, you may have weeks or even months to put something together. Then by all means use their expertise, and study their methods for those occasions when you have to write the treatment yourself.

THE FIVE-POINT TREATMENT

Writing a video treatment takes little more than common sense and a flexible format that can be employed from program to program. Condense your project into the five Ws listed below:

1. *Define your goals.*

   - Who will watch the video?
   - When will the audience watch the program?
   - Where will the audience watch the program?
   - What is the program's purpose?
   - Why is this program important?

This is the nucleus of your production. Using the information given to you during the first meeting, separate the video into basic categories:

2. *Provide specific information about your program.*

   - Program type (new product introduction; documentary; training)
   - Audience (sales representatives; community leaders; customer service agents)
   - Purpose (to inform; to persuade; to instruct)
   - Format: 3/4-inch master for VHS dubs
   - Length (5–20 minutes, depending on program type)
   - Budget: $1,500–$2,000 per finished minute of program

Three-quarter-inch videotape is an industry standard for taping and editing. Production companies also work in Betacam and Super VHS, but for now stick with the 3/4-inch format (for your information, "3/4-inch" refers to the width of the tape; VHS tape is often called "1/2-inch"). You won't know what format you'll eventually use until you talk to the production company.

"Dubs" refer to program copies for distribution to offices or individuals. Even if you don't need to use a duplication service for this particular project, leave the option open. Someone in your organization might come up with another use for the program later on and will want to know if copies can be made available.

As for program length, use the guide from Chapter 1 to set your parameters. A range of 3–6 minutes for a new product introduction, for example, not only leaves the program open to creative interpretation by the scriptwriter and director, but also helps to establish a working budget. Also, expand on the purpose of the program. Think about your objectives and goals and provide a brief explanation of what the program will ultimately accomplish.

I said earlier that the average video program costs $1,500–$2,000 per completed minute, but until you receive a bid from a production company, you won't know for sure exactly how much your program will cost. This is where program length comes into play. A quick calculation shows that a six-minute video will cost around $12,000. Always estimate the highest amount. If you do that, the production bid you agree to should come very close to your projection. If the bid turns out to be more than you expected, it may be because the production company included optional services you may not need or want that can be dropped to keep the program within a reasonable budget.

Now make a list of the outside services you intend to use. There's no need to fill in names right now because you haven't talked to anyone yet.

3. *List the people and services involved in your project.*

- Scriptwriter
- Production company
- Producer
- Director
- Talent
- Editor
- Duplicator
- Distributor

A production company often handles arrangements for talent, sets, tape stock, equipment rentals, editing time, and duplication, so you might want to modify this list later on. The house producer may also double as director or editor. As you gain production experience, you can arrange services such as talent and program duplication separately.

That takes care of your program's technical considerations. The next section deals with production deadlines:

4. *When will project events take place?*

- Program treatment
- Script draft
- Final script
- Pre-production meetings
- Studio date(s)
- Location date(s)
- Edit date(s)
- Final presentation
- Duplication
- Distribution

Pre-production encompasses time spent with a production company making decisions regarding the script, talent, location and studio taping, editing, and visual elements. Again, there's no need to fill in these events until later.

The final page of a treatment presents the synopsis, a compact version of the program's content. Working from your meeting notes and other information, formulate the synopsis as follows:

5. *Create a broad outline for the synopsis.*

Part 1:

- What does the audience need to know?
- Introduce the subject.
- State the company's role in the subject.

Part 2:

- What makes this topic special?
- What will it cover?
- List/show/explain program points.

Part 3:

- Reiterate your purpose in presenting the program.
- Highlight the company's commitment to excellence.
- Reinforce audience need to take action.

In other words—

Part 1: State the problem and the solution.

Part 2: Explain how the solution works.

Part 3: Tell what to expect from the solution.

Or, as a trainer once explained to me: tell them what you're going to do, do it, then tell them what you did.

Finally, write a note to yourself, headed "Home Office Participants." List everyone involved in the project, from those providing information to those granting approvals. This will serve as your in-house directory.

With your categories established and defined, and your meeting notes worked into a thumbnail sketch of the program's content, assemble them into an orderly report. [See figure 3.1.]

DEVELOPING A PRODUCTION SCHEDULE

Handing in a neatly typed treatment is not enough. Once it is read, someone is bound to say, "It looks great, but when is all this going to happen?" The project needs a timetable.

Trying to think weeks and months ahead of time is overwhelming at first—especially with so many elements to coordinate—but events are manageable. In fact, schedules do more than pacify time-conscious executives.

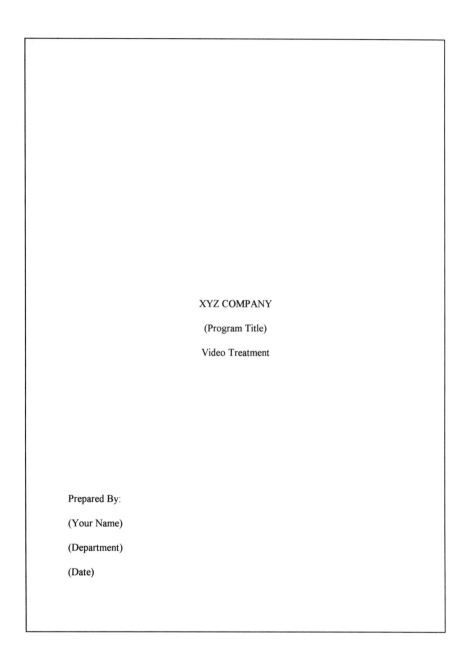

XYZ COMPANY

(Program Title)

Video Treatment

Prepared By:

(Your Name)

(Department)

(Date)

Figure 3.1   Sample Treatment Format

XYZ Company

(Program Title)

Video Treatment

Purpose: To introduce the benefits and features of (product name) and to inspire a national sales effort.

Audience: Sales Representatives.

Program Type: New product introduction.

Format: 3/4-Inch Master for VHS dubs.

Length: 3-6 minutes.

Budget: To be determined.

Production Services

Scriptwriter:

Production Company:

Director:

Talent:

Duplication:

Production Schedule

Treatment:

Script Drafts:

Figure 3.1 Sample Treatment Format *(continued)*

Final Script:

Pre-Production Meetings:

Studio Dates:

Location Dates:

Edit Dates:

Presentation:

Duplication:

Program Synopsis

XYZ Company is proud to introduce an exciting and innovative product, one designed to respond to the consumer's changing needs while giving you the commissions you deserve.

It's called (product name), and it combines a reliable, traditional design with the competitive, cost-conscious price consumers are looking for...

Giving you sales opportunities like never before!

In the past, there were very few products that offered long-term performance. They were reliable in their own way, but they never quite fit in with the consumer's changing needs, especially in an uncertain economy.

Figure 3.1 Sample Treatment Format *(continued)*

That's why XYZ Company committed its resources and talent to developing a product consumers can grow with, backed by service they can trust.

Let's see how (product) works.

(Briefly describe the main features and benefits of the product. Highlight key selling points. Touching on product basics, show how it works. Leave all exceptions and exclusions out).

The innovative features you've just seen make (product) the only choice for years to come. With (list three top features), (product) will come through time and time again!

XYZ Company is ready to back you with an exciting portfolio of sales material. In addition, inventory and shipping have been streamlined to provide you with the best possible service.

We think you'll agree that (product) is sophisticated yet simple, an idea that works for your clients in many ways. More important, it adds another powerful product to your portfolio!

Figure 3.1   Sample Treatment Format *(continued)*

What a Production Schedule Will Do for You

- A schedule provides concrete goals. It makes the production real. You've moved beyond talking about what's needed and when; now the video is underway and it has a definite date of completion.
- When you submit scripts, demo reels, and the finished program for review and approval, a schedule clears the way. That is, if you say that a script will arrive for review next Friday morning, management will make time for it. Even if executives are out of town, you can always use a fax machine or express delivery service to keep them informed.
- Having a schedule makes it easier to obtain print materials, answers to questions, and information. No one wants a production to be late; at least, no one wants to be held responsible for making the production late.

Any delays in scripting, production and editing, or approvals are absorbed by a good schedule. For this reason, leave production holes—vacant days—in the calendar to provide a cushion in the event of late scripts, missing persons, and unnatural disasters. Aside from supporting the overall structure of the schedule, holes also give you time to gather visual elements and stay in touch with key personnel.

All schedules begin with the delivery of content. Once you have all the necessary information to get the video started, set your production calendar for eight weeks. If no information is available and you have to do the research yourself, add another two weeks. This seems like a long time to gather information, but time is limited. You have other job duties to fulfill; you have to wait until marketing can get back to you with some answers; a customer service manager doesn't have time right now to sit down with you. The reasons are as varied as your business.

Let's go back to the last section for a moment to review our production deadlines:

Program treatment

Script draft

Final script

Pre-production meetings

Studio date(s)

Location date(s)

Edit date(s)

Final presentation

Duplication

Distribution

Now recall the weekly production assignments we discussed in Chapter 1:

2–3 weeks for information gathering, scripting, and approvals

2–3 weeks for production and post-production

1 week for viewing and changes

1 week for duplication and distribution

If you plugged these assignments into an eight-week calendar, the schedule would look like Figure 3.2. This doesn't tell you very much, however. You need to be more specific. Events must be clearly established.

Every production week has its own activities. Adapt the following model to your own needs.

Eight Week Production Calendar

Sun	Mon	Tues	Wed	Thurs	Fri	Sat
	1	2	3	4	5	6
7	8	9	10	11	12	13
14	15	16	17	18	19	20

Scriptwriting

21	22	23	24	25	26	27
28	29	30	31	1	2	3
4	5	6	7	8	9	10

Production/Post-Production

11	12	13	14	15	16	17

Viewing/Approvals/Changes

18	19	20	21	22	23	24

Duplication/Distribution

Figure 3.2   General Production Calendar

Production Week #1: August 1–5

Monday 1: Meet with company personnel to discuss project.

Tuesday 2: Write treatment/locate production services.

Wednesday 3: Call scriptwriters and production companies for sample scripts, demo reels, and rate sheets.

Friday 5: Review scripts/demo reels/rate sheets.

If program content was provided at the meeting, the first thing to do after writing up the treatment is to locate some scriptwriters and production companies. There are many ways to go about this:

- Consult a creative directory or source book.
- Call a company already doing video and ask for a recommendation.
- Contact a writers' association.
- Call a TV station and ask for a referral.

Scriptwriters are very accommodating. Competition is fierce, so many will hand-deliver, fax, or overnight their samples. You won't be waiting very long for results.

Ask each scriptwriter for three samples, a resumé, and a rate sheet. Narrow your search to at least three writers who are familiar with your industry and the subject matter. Scripts will arrive within a day or two. Be sure to make copies for others to look at.

Use these same sources to locate at least three production companies. Call and ask for the following:

- A demo reel
- A list of clients
- A rate sheet
- A basic bid for production services based on your projected program length, with a one-camera shoot, studio and editing time, and at least one narrator or two on-camera talent

If you see a lot of special effects and computer animation in a demo reel, chances are the production house likes to work with big budgets. A Fortune 500 client list will tell you the same thing. If you strike out on those two, the rate sheet and bid may be inconsequential. Of course, knowledge of your industry and the topic to be covered are also important.

Not all production companies will want to write up a quick bid because they'd rather meet with you to discuss the project and sell you on their services. Explain to them that at the moment you're only shopping around for a production house, with no immediate plans to set up meetings until you get an idea of how much everyone charges. This response ensures that a rate sheet will be included in their package of services.

Production Week #2: August 8–12

Monday 8: Call scriptwriter and production company to set up a meeting.
Tuesday 9: Meet with and hire scriptwriter.
Wednesday 10: Meet with and hire production company.
Friday 12: Review production bid.

If everyone took time to read the sample scripts and agrees on one writer, set an appointment to meet with him right away. The same goes for the production company. You can get the writer started immediately. Give him a deadline of one week for the first draft, and delivery of the final script a week after changes and approvals are received.

The staff of a production house will have to write up a formal bid. Discussing your program in greater detail will help them decide what equipment and services they'll use and when they'll be needed. Give them a day or two to check on the availability of studio and editing time and to submit their bid. Make copies for review and approval.

Production Week #3: August 15–19

Monday 15: Approve production bid/call production company in for pre-production meeting.
Tuesday 16: Receive first script draft.
Wednesday 17: Pre-production meeting with production company.
Friday 19: Send script changes to writer.

Week 3 consists of meetings. When you receive the first draft of the script, be sure to send a copy to the production company for scene assignments and to managers for review. Scene assignments are not set in stone, and the production company knows that. Giving the staff a draft to work from will give them a good idea what to expect from the production in terms of shooting schedules, locations, and equipment.

The pre-production meeting on Wednesday is when you'll begin to solidify your show. Aside from setting tentative studio, location, and editing dates, the house producer will also bring along talent photos and sometimes demo reels. Route all photos or copies of photos to key company personnel and if possible set up a separate meeting to watch or listen to demos.

Go over the script and talk about scenes that require special attention.

That attention can be anything from making sure a location shot includes the most up-to-date technology in use by your company to setting up a proper sales presentation. The house producer will make the appropriate notes and ask questions to get a feel for how your company works and what the audience will expect to see and learn.

Keep the program simple. A producer I worked with on several occasions provides a case in point. He was an incredibly talented and enthusiastic producer, ready to do whatever it took to make the program worthy of an Academy Award. When discussing a script, he would often get so excited by the material that he would launch into a litany of special effects and exotic locations we could use to "really punch up the visuals."

I'd let him ramble on as long as he wanted, then calmly remind him that we couldn't afford it—why don't we do this, instead? He'd sulk for a moment, agree that yeah, we could do that, then we'd move on until something else got him going again. I always enjoyed working with him, and our programs always turned out great, but if I hadn't maintained a simple approach to the production, there's no telling how much money we would have spent.

Managers will have a few days to look over the script. Consolidate their comments and suggestions into a single list, citing script page numbers and paragraphs, and send the list to the writer. If you're not sure what someone means by a particular comment, ask him for clarification or to provide corresponding information. A scriptwriter won't have much to work with if you say, "Include last year's European figures and manufacturing stats."

Production Week #4: August 22–26

Monday 22: Assemble visuals.

Wednesday 24: Pre-production meeting #2.

Friday 26: Final script delivered.

At this point your production schedule begins to open up. Assembling any visuals your company will provide—such as product brochures, training manuals, etc.—is an ongoing process that doesn't have to be done in one day. Should the script require shooting in different areas of the company, be sure you inform department managers when and where you'll be taping and whether you'll need to tape employees performing certain tasks in order to set up or explain a scene.

The second pre-production meeting on Wednesday is spent choosing talent and confirming production dates. Unless you really need to meet face-to-face, this can be done by phone. The house producer will probably have to get back to you to let you know if your chosen talent are free when you want them, so be sure to have backup candidates in mind.

Depending upon how quickly the writer works to incorporate any changes, a final draft is ready by Friday, if not before. Don't wait for additional comments before routing the script. Minor changes can be done within a day, and the production company will need to get the script to the talent.

Production Week #5: August 29–September 2

Tuesday 30: Studio taping.
Wednesday 31: Optional studio taping.
Thursday 1: Location taping.
Friday 2: Optional location taping.

The big week. Armed with the final script, you sit in on the taping sessions as producer and company specialist. It doesn't really matter what days of the week you agree on; you might require only one day in the studio and no location taping at all. An extra day or two gives you time to collect any last-minute visuals or to perform any of your regular job duties.

Production Week #6: September 5–9

Monday 5: Program editing.
Tuesday 6: Program editing.
Wednesday 7: Program editing.
Friday 9: Presentation and approval.

It takes no more than two days to edit a six-minute program, but schedule a third as a cushion. This leaves extra time in case the editing suite experiences mechanical failures or glitches leading to down time. When editing is complete, the production company will give you a copy of the program in whatever format you need (usually VHS) and keep the master.

The final presentation date is flexible. If those providing approvals can't get together on Friday, move the viewing date to the following Monday.

Company executives might prefer to have their own copy of the program to take home and watch at their leisure. Don't let this happen if you can help it, and certainly don't let it become a habit. Weekend promises to view a program are notorious for dismantling even the best schedule.

Individual showings of your program should be avoided. Getting everyone together at one time and place is not always easy to do, but it helps wrap up the program as soon as possible. You don't want to go running back and forth from office to office explaining how this person felt about it and what that person thought should be done to the soundtrack.

Production Week #7: September 12–16

Monday 12: Optional presentation and approval.

Tuesday 13: Program changes.

Thursday 15: Optional viewing and approval.

Friday 16: Program duplication.

Any possible changes to the program are discussed during pre-production meetings. An editing suite can be held without a firm commitment, so there's no need to worry about paying for studio time if changes aren't necessary.

Minor errors and alterations take only a few hours or a day to correct. Page after page of script rewrites will require bringing the talent back into the studio for re-recording or taping, adding at least another week to the schedule.

Production Week #8: September 19–23

Monday 19–Thursday 22: Program duplication.

Friday 23: Program distribution.

Duplication time depends on program length and the number of copies needed. The production company or duplicating service can give you an estimate.

In the meantime, talk to your company mail room manager about shipping methods and cost. He might have to order special boxes or envelopes. One company I worked for sent its tapes out in its weekly payroll mail pouches, thereby cutting separate shipping costs.

The schedule now looks like Figure 3.3. Notice where production holes come into play. In addition, many of your actions will only take a few hours out of the day, which opens up even more time. Again, this is only a model. You may find you need an extra day or two to accomplish certain tasks, which is why production holes are so important.

Now fill in the deadlines on page one of your treatment:

Script treatment: (Date of submission)

Script draft: Tuesday August 16

Final script: Friday August 26

Pre-production meetings: Wednesday August 17 and Wednesday August 24

Studio date(s): Tuesday August 30 and/or Wednesday August 31

Production Month #1

Sunday	Monday	Tuesday	Wednesday	Thursday	Friday	Saturday
	1 Meet with company personnel to discuss video	*2* Write treatment/Locate Production Services	*3* Call scriptwriters and production companies for sample scripts, demo reels, and rate sheets	*4*	*5* Review sample scripts and production company demo reels	*6*
7	*8* Call scriptwriters for bids/Set up meetings with production companies	*9* Meet with and hire scriptwriter	*10* Meet with production companies/ Ask for project bid	*11*	*12* Review production bids	*13*
14	*15* Approve production bid/Set up pre-production meeting with production company	*16* Receive first script draft/Route for comments	*17* Meet with production company	*18*	*19* Give script changes to scriptwriter	*20*
21	*22* Assemble visuals	*23*	*24* Pre-production meeting	*25*	*26* Final script delivered	*27*
28	*29*	*30* Studio taping	*31* Optional studio taping			

Figure 3.3 Complete Production Calendar. Printed by Calendar Creator Plus.

Location date(s): Thursday September 1 and/or Friday September 2
Edit dates: Monday September 5 through Wednesday September 7
Final presentation: Friday September 9 or Monday September 12
Duplication: Friday September 16 through Thursday September 22
Distribution: Friday September 23

Production Month #2

Sunday	Monday	Tuesday	Wednesday	Thursday	Friday	Saturday
				1 Location taping	2 Optional location taping	3
4	5 Program editing	6 Program editing	7 Optional program editing	8	9 Final Presentation and approval	10
11	12 Optional presentation and approval	13 Optional progam changes in editing	14	15 Second optional viewing and approvals	16 Master tape in for duplication	17
18	19 Program duplication	20	21	22	23 Program distribution	24
25	26	27	28	29	30	

Figure 3.3   Complete Production Calendar. Printed by Calendar Creator Plus. *(continued)*

The program change date is left out of the treatment for practical reasons. Script approval implies early acceptance of the final program. Only spelling mistakes or incorrectly identified items necessitate a second trip to the editing suite.

This date is set during pre-production only as a contingency. It is not an expectation or a matter to discuss with management. If you tell managers—even indirectly—that you expect problems with the final program, they will come to expect it, too. The final presentation then becomes nothing more than an open forum for redoing the project.

As soon as you get the program approved, call the production company to start the duplication process.

Useful as it is, a treatment does have its negative side. If the finished program looks any different from what you developed in the treatment, approvals may be difficult to obtain. You can prevent this by making it clear that the report is merely a foundation to build on, and that additional details will be provided as work progresses.

Another technique for creating a schedule involves counting backward. If your sales meeting takes place at the end of June, you can count back 8 weeks to determine deadlines. I can't recommend this approach; it may work for some types of programs, but it creates unwelcome pressures. For example, if you count back and find you've got an extra week for others to provide content, look out—you may not get it because the need is not perceived to be immediate. Always start your production calendar count from the delivery of content.

Submit the treatment and production calendar and request weekly update meetings to keep the lines of communication open. If there are any changes or problems, everyone will know about it, and there will be fewer surprises down the road.

Upcoming chapters take an in-depth look at the services you'll be working with for the next two months. Before then, however, you need to manage your production by learning how to manage your time.

AT THIS STAGE OF THE PRODUCTION PLANNING PROCESS YOU SHOULD

- Condense your notes into distinct production categories.
- Create a list of production deadlines.
- Write a program synopsis.
- Develop a production schedule.
- Fill in production dates in your treatment and submit the finished report for approval.

4

Managing Your Time

Developing a video production calendar is essential in terms of keeping assignments and deadlines on track, but without a personal calendar, you may find your new video duties constantly at odds with your regular job duties.

Whenever you take on a video assignment, scheduling conflicts are inevitable. What seems an exciting diversion from your everyday responsibilities is tempered by a sudden rush of panic that unless you have extensive training as a professional juggler, your days are going to get very crazy, very fast. Managing your time, you realize, is the only way you'll be able to meet your goals.

A perfect example of this problem was illustrated in a television commercial that ran several years ago. A salesman sitting at his desk gets a call from the boss. "You want me to go to Chicago on Wednesday? I can do that. Atlanta on Thursday? I can do that. Los Angeles and San Francisco on Friday? I can do that." Then he hangs up the phone. "How am I going to do that?"

The best way to keep your days free from clutter and confusion is the simplest: take a pad of paper and a pen, sit down, and establish a list of priorities.

LIST ONE: YOUR JOB DESCRIPTION

Day-to-day activities. What assignments are you expected to complete on a daily basis? Are there certain times of the day when you need to complete specific tasks?

Projects. List all of the projects you're currently working on, as well as all upcoming assignments. How far along are you on your ongoing projects, and how long do you expect upcoming projects to last?

Meetings. Some companies and organizations have regular meeting days to discuss business or to coordinate activities. When do these meetings take place, and how long do they usually last?

Classes. Are you currently involved in any training sessions? How important are they to your job?

Vendors. Do you maintain regular contact with reps from the services you use? List these services and any upcoming meeting dates.

Seminars. Out-of-office seminars are often set up months in advance. Will you be out of town for more than a day or two?

Miscellaneous activities. Do you perform community or charity work on behalf of your company? Are there any medical appointments to consider? Personal time and/or vacation coming up?

LIST TWO: VIDEO DUTIES

Level of involvement. What step or steps in the production process are you responsible for?

Specific duties. Within your level of involvement, list all of the actions you need to perform. Are you responsible for gathering information for the script-writer? Calling around for production company demo reels and rate sheets? Assembling visuals for the studio shoot? Everything?

Personnel. Are you working on your own, or are you working with others on the same duties? Make a list of their responsibilities. To whom will you be reporting?

Now that you have your two lists, compare your regular job duties with those dates on the production calendar when you're expected to perform a video function. It's not a pretty sight, is it? Chances are you show conflicts all over the place. How can you possibly sit in on an editing session when you're supposed to be in Vancouver for a conference? When are you going to find the time to review sample scripts from freelance writers when you're going to be stuck in one meeting after another on the same day?

There are no easy answers to these conflicts. Getting the video done on time is the most important thing you have to do right now, and while no one wants to worry about falling behind in his daily workload, there are steps you can take to coordinate your combined duties to minimize problems.

REEVALUATE YOUR JOB DUTIES

Go back to the first list you made and think about what you can do to make your job easier.

Day-to-day activities. Can some of your daily assignments be given to others or can you have the number of assignments reduced? If you spend a lot of time on the phone with branch offices or clients, is there someone else who can take over some or all of those calls? As for assignments carried out at certain times of the day, see if they can be performed at an earlier or later time.

Projects. How important are the projects you're working on? Can they be delayed a week or two while you're working on the video? Some of your upcoming projects will last several months. Can they be reassigned or your involvement in them shifted to encompass some other task?

Meetings. What meetings can be missed? If you're expected to report on your department's activities, ask if you can turn in a written report instead.

Classes. There are two types of job training sessions: those offered in-house on a continuous basis, and those conducted at a remote site on a monthly or quarterly basis. Have you started your classes yet? If not, try to reschedule them. Dropping out of a class you're four sessions into is more difficult, especially if it involves training on something critical to the performance of your job. How many more classes do you have to attend? Are there similar classes offered on a different day or time that you can join?

Vendors. What vendors are important enough to see? Perhaps you're meeting with a printer to look at paper samples for your next newsletter. A graphic artist wants to show you how the direct mail piece will look. These appointments can be moved around to accommodate your needs. The vendors you can cancel or delay are those who want to introduce themselves and their services. Call them and put these meetings on hold.

Seminars. The problem with seminars is that they're arranged and paid for months ahead of time, and like any training class, the session or sessions may have a direct bearing on your job. If you're going to be out of the office during a critical time in the production schedule, someone else will have to take your place, whether it's out on location or in the editing suite.

Miscellaneous activities. Personal time off can be pushed back to another day, but vacation time is another matter. That resort you booked eight months ago required a sizeable deposit, the balance is due soon, and you haven't taken a vacation in three years. Video—what video? If you have vacation time looming in the near future, make sure your boss and everyone else associated with the project knows about it. This information may require bringing in an assistant to work with you, someone who can take over for you while you're away.

Communities and charities rely on volunteers to help make their programs successful, and your efforts reflect well on your company or organization. If you feel strongly about the time you spend with them, work out an arrangement to move your schedule to evenings or weekends. Medical appointments can be similarly rearranged.

So far I've kept the discussion of managing your time limited to rearranging your daily schedule to accommodate your video schedule, but that doesn't mean you should sacrifice everything for the sake of this one project. Production calendars are meant to establish a flexible timetable of events, not an immutable law. If you need to move back a meeting date with the scriptwriter or move up the dates of your editing sessions, by all means do so.

What's important is that if you have serious conflicts between your regular job duties and those brought on by video, talk to your manager or whoever assigned you the project and make these problems known. It could be that you were inadvertently assigned too many video duties without any thought given to that big marketing project you'll be in charge of next week. Talking about it helps others see that you can only do so much. You want the video to be successful, but not at the expense of having a negative impact on the company's bottom line.

REEVALUATE YOUR VIDEO DUTIES

To help resolve some of your scheduling conflicts, there are some things you can do to minimize the amount of time spent putting your production together.

1.   When contacting scriptwriters, production houses, talent agencies, duplicators, or any other service you'll be working with, always make your calls first thing in the morning.

From time to time I worked with people who took a lackadaisical attitude when it came to making calls. They would wait until after lunch or a coffee break, or put it off until the next day. Sometimes they lucked out and were able to get what they needed right away, and other times they left a huge, gaping hole in the production calendar where an editing session should have been.

There's enough to deal with in a production without making it harder on everyone else, so don't wait to make your calls. For most professionals in the video community, every day starts early and ends late. If you wait until three o'clock in the afternoon to request a rate sheet or get an answer to a question, you probably won't get a response until the next day. By making your calls early, you stand a better chance of reaching your contact directly or having her get back to you sooner. And by getting a jump on your calls, you'll leave a lot more room in your schedule for other job duties.

2.   Be clear about what you want and when you want it. Many of the problems in video production come from a basic lack of communication. When a writer says he can have that script for you early next week, ask for a specific day and time. Early next week can mean anything from Monday morning to

Wednesday. When the house producer says she may be able to get those editing dates you wanted, ask for a confirmation as soon as possible.

When a company I produced news programs for wanted to bring in some talent for auditions, I called my contact at the talent agency and set up an entire morning's worth of readings. In the meantime, I rescheduled some meetings, put some other work on hold to set aside time for the auditions, and prepared the studio for taping.

No one showed up. By ten-thirty it was obvious that a dozen people could not have possibly lost their way, so I called the agency and asked where everyone was.

"Was that today?" my contact asked.

"Sure was," I said, my head about to explode.

The rep checked his book and apologized. It seems he was working on a similar assignment at the same time, and by mistake switched the schedules, no doubt sending a dozen people to a company that had no idea they were coming. We had to set up another day, not an easy thing with so many people involved.

What went wrong? I called to set up the auditions, and the rep confirmed the date and time each person would come in for a reading. It should have worked. My mistake was not calling a day or two before the auditions to follow up, and I learned from that experience not to take anything for granted.

3.   If you're dissatisfied because you're having a difficult time getting hold of people, or because they're being vague about whether or not they'll be able to do something for you, be honest about it. No matter how many shows or scripts someone is working on, your project is just as important and should be treated as such.

There are many times when a producer or service rep on the other end of the line assumes you know as much as she does about the business or understand the jargon of the industry. If you feel your conversation is getting bogged down in confusion, stop and go over everything again until you understand what's going on. This saves on the number of calls you have to make trying to get a handle on what your production needs.

Early on in my corporate video career I was given the assignment to "call" a show for a national sales conference to be attended by company employees, sales agents and their spouses, executives, stockholders, and government dignitaries. Until that moment I had been responsible for writing and producing a video, a 24-projector slide show, and speeches, but calling a show was something else.

What that meant was sitting off to one side of a massive ballroom making sure each part of the conference ran like clockwork. Reading from a lengthy script—and wearing a headset that felt like a block of concrete was sitting on my head—I had to tell the people working the spotlights when to follow someone across the stage and when to stay put; I had to let the projector operators know when we were about to start the multi-projector presentation; I had to make sure that audio levels were consistently balanced between the singers and the speakers.

There was a lot to do, and I had never called a show in my life.

The producer working the computer console next to me was an old hand at corporate shows and had been hired by the production company to make sure that the two dozen projectors stayed in sync. He was also somewhat distant and cool toward me. There was no way I was going to call this show on my own, so before we sat down to go through the script I told him right away that I had never called a show in my life and that I could certainly use his help.

From that moment on he was a different person. He called the more complicated routines in the show for me, and whenever we had a few minutes between musical numbers or speakers he would explain to me how to keep everything in line, how to anticipate and get people ready. He had assumed I knew what I was doing, so he never bothered to get involved in the production beyond his own assignment. It was a great experience for me, and I think in the end he appreciated my honesty. All I had to do was ask.

A FINAL WORD ABOUT TIME MANAGEMENT

Managing your time does not have to be complicated or career-threatening. By making a list of job responsibilities and thinking through the effort it takes to get those jobs done, you will often find that what seems insurmountable at first is really nothing more than looking at it from a different perspective.

The trick is to be flexible about what you can and can't do. If a sudden hole pops up in your video production calendar—the writer delivers the script two days ahead of time, the producer tells you that you'll only need one day of location taping—take the time to get caught up on those client phone calls or files, or start something new you can finish in a day. You'll be surprised at how quickly you'll adapt.

AT THIS STAGE OF THE PRODUCTION PLANNING PROCESS YOU SHOULD

- Make a list of your regular job duties and your new video duties.
- Compare your day-to-day assignments with your production calendar.
- Make adjustments to both schedules to maximize your time.
- Inform managers and others associated with the project if problems arise or conflicts cannot be easily resolved.

5

Get Organized: Using Forms to Create a Production Book

When I produced my first video, I didn't really understand what I had gotten myself into until I tried to recall just exactly what had been done when, and where, and at what cost in terms of time and money. At that point, as I sifted through an expandable file folder filled with pages of notes, scribbles on the backs of torn sheets of paper and gum wrappers, and enigmatic reminders in newspaper margins, I decided that there must be a better way of keeping my sanity and my productions on track. What I needed was a systematic way of documenting my thoughts and actions while at the same time keeping the business end of my productions in check. After all, I was supposed to know what I was doing.

No one in this business was born with an innate sense of how to organize all of the elements of production. The process has to be learned. Every production house, communications department, and independent producer has, over time and with experience, developed a method of documenting the people, resources, costs, and time involved in the making of a video. The International Television Association, for example, publishes a handbook of forms, a collection of contributions from companies around the country, covering every aspect of video production. No two forms are the same, and there's no reason why they should be. Every approach to video demands its own standard. What you need to do is determine what standard works best for you.

FILE IT!

Aside from the obvious result of maintaining one source for all of your production information, consider the long-term effects organizing your projects will have:

- An organized production book gives you a solid base from which to start the next time you produce a video. You'll know exactly who to contact for your needs.
- It provides valuable information as to what to do or bring to a meeting, studio, or editing suite.
- It gives you easy access to phone numbers and production costs.
- It shows you how and where you can cut costs. (Would you consider employing non-union talent for your next show? Did you order too many copies of your program?)
- It points out the strengths and weaknesses in your production schedule. (What worked and what didn't? You scheduled enough time for scripting and pre-production meetings, but approvals were slow in coming and occasionally set you back. What can you do next time to make your schedule more efficient?)
- It breaks down production services in such a way that others within your department or company can see and understand the time and expense that video production demands.

WHAT SHOULD A PRODUCTION BOOK CONTAIN?

The forms found at the end of this chapter were created with basic production considerations in mind. Use them to develop your own forms. However you use them, keep in mind that every production book should contain the following:

- Program treatment
- Final script
- Photocopies of talent headshots (if you use more than one person, note what role each person played)
- Production calendar
- Whatever forms included in this chapter pertain to your production
- Copies of bids, contracts, invoices, and orders
- Program evaluation summary (to be covered later in this book)

To make it easier to find the information you need, color code each page or section, have an in-house graphics department design separate pages for each service rendered, use dividers to set each section apart, or create subdirectories within your word processing program to develop and store individual production documents.

The best way to keep your productions within arm's reach is to use a three-ring binder. That way you can carry your project along with you while in a meeting, out on location, or in a studio. When you finish your show, label the binder and keep it handy on a bookshelf for easy reference.

CREATING SEPARATE VIDEO FILES

As you utilize various services and get your name on mailing lists, you should also create and maintain separate files covering other aspects of production. These include:

- Yearly project summaries
- Talent photos and resumés
- Sales and services literature
- Catalogs
- Sample scripts from freelance scriptwriters
- Magazine articles
- Company logos and artwork

There are other production activities you should consider as well:

- Start a phone book of regularly used services.
- Build a library of audio and video demo reels.
- Make others in your organization aware of seminars, open houses, and training tapes that are available.
- Route video magazines to managers who might be interested in producing videos.
- Start a contact list of other producers and companies who are producing videos. You never know when they can offer advice or solve a problem.

WHAT FORMS ARE INCLUDED IN THIS CHAPTER?

In designing the following forms, I kept their formats simple so that you can see what information is essential to a production while leaving open your own needs.

Yearly video project summary. (Figure 5.1) If you produce more than one video per year, it's a good idea to generate a summary showing your involvement in the process. This is important if your primary job has nothing to do with video, as it may be necessary to rewrite your job description to reflect a change in your overall duties.

Project cost summary. (Figure 5.2) All video production books contain a list of expenditures. Including copies of itemized invoices provides additional details should you need to refer to the number of hours charged for editing or how much you were billed for customized tape labels.

Production company. (Figure 5.3) This form has many uses. First, it provides vital information on the company used, who your contacts were, and any notes relating to your dealings with them. If you use the same production house more than once but work with other staff members, you can compare their styles and abilities. Should you use different production companies from program to program, you won't have to rely on memory to tell you which people went out of their way for you and who was difficult to reach when you needed to confirm location dates.

Production schedule. (Figure 5.4) Make copies of this form and pass them around to everyone associated with your project. It's not only a good way to remind those granting approvals that deadlines need to be kept, but also to let them know when you'll be out of the office. That way they won't have to constantly refer to your program treatment to figure out why you're not answering your phone.

Talent agency. (Figure 5.5) Personal impressions in dealing with a talent agent should be noted. Was the agent easy to work with? Did she have a variety of talent to choose from? Were her rates reasonable?

Department meeting notes. (Figure 5.6) Always document who attended meetings, what was said, and what was decided. Use a pad of paper for these notes, then organize and condense your material into a brief report.

Pre-production notes. (Figure 5.7) When you meet with a production company, you'll discuss many topics and make many decisions, so have multiple copies of this form on hand. If there's a change in location sites or talent, list the reasons for these changes. Use a separate form for each phone call. Also, get a feel for the house producer's approach to the program. Was she enthusiastic about your project, did she offer suggestions on ways to give your program a special look?

Production notes. (Figure 5.8) All productions are two-way streets. The production company expects you to deliver reliable and accurate information, and you expect the production company to take that information and create an effective program. But that's not the end of the creative process. Once shooting begins, suggestions and ideas on how a scene should be played out require your input. The house producer may ask if your company has a logo she can use. Small details inevitably crop up, so be prepared.

Props. (Figure 5.9) If you borrow plaques, lamps, trinkets, or set pieces from other departments or companies, keep track of them. You don't want someone calling up later on, asking where his award is.

Location report. (Figure 5.10) All location shoots are unique. The weather may play a factor, or a sudden power outage may derail an otherwise perfect taping. Did the talent read well? Did you feel the director captured the essence of the script? Were there any problems?

Post-production report. (Figure 5.11) A good editing facility can make or break a project. Did you feel your opinion was important? Was the equipment working properly? Did the editor make suggestions that enhanced your program? These are important considerations. Once you find an editor who is totally responsive to your needs, you may never want another.

Equipment rental. (Figure 5.12) This form applies to those producers who contract outside services for all their needs, or for those services not provided by the production house. Pay special attention to customer service, prices, and equipment quality.

Travel. (Figure 5.13) At some point, you may find yourself traveling to another city for location shooting. If your company or organization reimburses you for your expenses, attach copies of all receipts.

Presentation. (Figure 5.14) When you make your final presentation to managers or other decision-makers, you'll no doubt have a lot of comments to deal with. Just as you did with your meeting notes, use a pad of paper to record their thoughts. Their impressions will give you a good idea of how to approach or improve future productions.

Program duplication. (Figure 5.15) A production company often makes arrangements for duplication, but if you do it on your own, it's important that you keep close tabs on when your program was submitted and when the copies were delivered. How did the copies look?

Program distribution. (Figure 5.16) Program copies sent to offices or individuals should always be tracked, especially if they have to arrive for a special event or on a specific calendar date. (Did you use the company mailroom, or did you use a packaging and delivery service?)

Miscellaneous expenditures. (Figure 5.17) There will be times when your shows require purchasing items on your own. For example, I produced a Thanksgiving program that needed some holiday decorations. It made more sense to walk down to the corner store and buy the decorations myself than to have the production company purchase them for me.

Take the time to get organized. There's no excuse for executing a sloppy production if you really care about what you're doing. Your efforts will show. It seems time-consuming at first, but the sooner you establish a definitive way of documenting your productions, the easier it will become later on.

AT THIS STAGE OF THE PRODUCTION PLANNING PROCESS YOU SHOULD

- Consider the advantages of assembling your own production book.
- Use a three-ring binder to keep your notes, forms, and documents in one place.
- Create separate files containing information relating to video.
- Take the opportunity to start your own library of demo tapes.
- Make others in your organization aware of seminars, training tapes, and other video services.

VIDEO PROJECT SUMMARY
(YEAR)

Project #	Description	Created	Completed

Figure 5.1 Yearly Video Project Summary

VIDEO PROJECT COST SUMMARY

(PROJECT # /DESCRIPTION)

	Description/Quantity	Cost
Scriptwriter		
Production Company		
Talent		
Editing		
Duplication		
Distribution		
	Total	

	Description/Quantity	Cost
Equipment Rentals		
Tape Stock		
Travel		
Miscellaneous		
	Total	

TOTAL PROJECT COST	

Figure 5.2 Project Cost Summary

PRODUCTION COMPANY

(PROJECT # /DESCRIPTION)

Company Name:

Address:

City/State/Zip:

Phone:

Fax:

Contact:

Notes:

Figure 5.3   Production Company

PRODUCTION SCHEDULE

(PROJECT # /DESCRIPTION)

Treatment:

Script Draft:

Final Script:

Location Date(s):

Studio Date(s):

Editing Date(s):

Final Presentation:

Duplication:

Distribution/Show Date(s):

Notes:

Figure 5.4 Production Schedule

TALENT

(PROJECT # /DESCRIPTION)

Talent:

Rate:

Agency:

Address:

City/State/Zip:

Phone:

Fax:

Contact:

Notes:

Figure 5.5 Talent Agency

DEPARTMENT MEETING NOTES

(PROJECT # /DESCRIPTION)

Date:

Attendees:

Subject:

Notes:

Figure 5.6 Department Meeting Notes

PRE-PRODUCTION NOTES

(PROJECT # /DESCRIPTION)

Date:

Attendees:

Subject:

Notes:

Figure 5.7 Pre-production Notes

PRODUCTION NOTES

(PROJECT # /DESCRIPTION)

Date:

Attendees:

Subject:

Notes:

Figure 5.8 Production Notes

PROPS

(PROJECT # /DESCRIPTION)

Date	Description	Received	Returned

Notes:

Figure 5.9 Props

LOCATION REPORT

(PROJECT # /DESCRIPTION)

Date:

Script Page(s):

Location:

Production Hours:

Talent:

Notes:

Figure 5.10 Location Report

POST-PRODUCTION REPORT

(PROJECT # /DESCRIPTION)

Date:

Editing Facility:

Editor:

Company:

Address:

City/State/Zip:

Phone:

Fax:

Contact:

Notes:

Figure 5.11 Post-production Report

EQUIPMENT RENTAL

(PROJECT # /DESCRIPTION)

Date:

Item:

Cost:

Vendor:

Address:

City/State/Zip:

Phone:

Fax:

Contact:

Delivered:

Returned:

Notes:

Figure 5.12 Equipment Rental

TRAVEL

(PROJECT # /DESCRIPTION)

Date:

Location:

Purpose:

Script Page(s):

Talent:

Mileage:

Airfare:

Departure/Return:

Hotel:

Breakfast/Lunch/Dinner:

Phone:

Miscellaneous:

Figure 5.13 Travel

PRESENTATION

(PROJECT # /DESCRIPTION)

Date:

Location:

Attendees:

Notes:

Figure 5.14 Presentation

PROGRAM DUPLICATION

(PROJECT # /DESCRIPTION)

Date:

Vendor:
Address:
City/State/Zip:
Phone:
Fax:
Contact:

Number of Copies/Cost:
Number of Tape Labels/Cost:

Date Master Tape Submitted:
Date Duplication Completed:
Copies Delivered/Cost:

Figure 5.15 Program Duplication

PROGRAM DISTRIBUTION

(PROJECT # /DESCRIPTION)

Date:

Number of Copies Mailed:

Format:

Carrier:

Address:

City/State/Zip:

Phone:

Fax:

Contact:

Date Sent:

Cost:

Figure 5.16 Program Distribution

MISCELLANEOUS EXPENDITURES

(PROJECT # /DESCRIPTION)

Date:

Item:

Cost:

Purpose:

Vendor:

Address:

City/State/Zip:

Phone:

Fax:

Contact:

Notes:

Figure 5.17   Miscellaneous Expenditures

STEP 2

Pre-Production

6

The Scriptwriter and the Script

The key to the ultimate success of your video comes long before any studio lights are turned on and the tape starts to roll. Before the special effects, before the award-winning performances and awe-inspiring camera shots, there is the script. Simply stated, you cannot make a good video from a weak script. Dazzling computer animation and expensive talent won't get your message across if the words aren't there.

Always strive for the best possible script. There are many fine, competent writers out there, but you will also find a plethora of pretenders who have no ear for the spoken word, no sense of rhythm and timing, and no respect for an audience. As a producer, your choice of a writer involves many considerations. Simply giving someone a break will cost you.

WHAT TO LOOK FOR IN A SCRIPTWRITER

Working with a scriptwriter can be a pleasurable and constructive experience, or it can be a nightmare. If there is any part of the production that can be considered the weak link, this is it.

It is very important to establish guidelines for choosing a writer. I like to use an "SPT" (SPOT) check:

Samples. A writer must have some knowledge of your business and the type of program you want to create. If you're producing a training program for a meat packing company, ask to see several training-oriented scripts relating to the food industry.

Price. How much do scriptwriters charge? There are two ways—by the final number of pages or per running minute of program. I know of very few writers who charge by the day or hour. Rates run anywhere from $200 per page/minute and up. A finished script runs approximately one minute per page.

Whatever rate or price you agree to, make sure you know exactly what you're paying for. Script rewrites, messenger services, long-distance phone calls, travel, and other expenses are not always included and may be billed separately.

Time. What kind of turnaround time can you expect? If a writer is well acquainted with your program type (training, documentary, sales), if content is delivered the same day as he's hired, and if there is no research time involved, it should take no more than a week for him to produce a first draft. A final script delivered within two weeks should not be a problem.

FINDING A SCRIPTWRITER

How do you know if a scriptwriter will meet your needs? Unless someone in your company has worked with a writer before and recommends his services, you won't know for sure until you make your own calls, analyze writing samples, and talk to her on an individual basis to discuss the project. You can, however, minimize any guesswork involved by using established sources:

1.   *Creative directory.* A standard creative directory ad looks much like Figure 6.1. True, you can't tell very much about the person, but you can get some indication of her experience, especially if she lists big-name clients.

Here is a sample of what today's writer is doing in the business world:

- Copywriting
- Lyrics
- Editorial
- Television
- Speeches
- Proposals
- Print
- Direct mail
- Brochures
- Audiovisual
- Film
- Live shows
- Theater
- Project consultation
- Filmstrips
- Multi-image

TED QUILLPEN

555/555-5555

1000 Main Street, Anywhere USA 10000-0001

Award-winning writer with a special flair for business needs

o   Scripts for video and audio-visual productions

o   Specializes in training, new product introductions, and executive messages

o   High quality and dependable work

o   Sample scripts available

I can meet your deadlines and your budget--Try Me!

Figure 6.1   Sample Scriptwriter Ad

- Radio
- Video

It's difficult to tell how good a scriptwriter is from a six- or eight-line ad, but as a rule any listing containing more than three or four of the above pegs the writer as a generalist. For now, stick with those who write scripts and nothing but scripts.

2.   *Writers' associations.* Professional organizations publish directories with a list of names and the specialties of their members, and are willing to help you find the person you need. If there's a local chapter of the organization, attend a meeting and get to know some of the players. Once you've contacted a professional organization, you'll find that writers will send you unsolicited scripts. Keep them on file. If you establish a collection of names and samples, it will be much easier to hire a writer for your next production.

3.   *Company recommendation.* A recommendation from another company can take you in many directions. You may not find the scriptwriter of your dreams the first time out, but certainly the quality of work recommended to

you has already been proven to others and will produce satisfying results. It can also lead you back through a creative directory or a professional organization.

Whatever source works best for you, call at least three writers. If they're within close proximity to your company, have them drop off their samples, rate sheet, and a sample contract. Many writers have their programs available on video. If they have a demo reel, ask to see it.

It should not take more than a day or two to get sample scripts. Read them carefully and take note of the following:

- Are program points clear and well presented?
- Is the writer comfortable using technical terms?
- Does the program move freely?

Also have your writers submit the names of companies they've worked for and call them. Find out what they were like to work with. Were there any problems? Were deadlines met? Were the companies satisfied with their work? How did they feel about the rates?

HIRING A SCRIPTWRITER

When everyone involved in your project has read through the sample scripts and watched any demo reels, choose the most promising writer and set up a meeting. You know the scriptwriter wants your business, so don't feel you need to talk about your project right away. In fact, if you talk about the program up front without learning anything about the writer, he may agree to anything.

The writer probably knows very little about you or your organization, so have him talk about his own experiences first. Ask him to describe what went into his scripts. Get a feel for his involvement. When he's through, have him tell you about the projects that were similar to what you're doing now.

Ask about turnaround time and rates. Say that you will be providing all the information and that you've already written a treatment. Does he have a problem with producing a first draft within one week and a final script within two?

It's best to define your expectations at the start. Your time is limited. If a scriptwriter is too busy or isn't sure if he can make a deadline, thank him and move on to the next candidate. Never let a scriptwriter tell you how to run your show. You are paying for his services. If he can't give you what you want, I guarantee you someone else will.

If the writer fits your needs, tell him about your company and the project you want to produce. Have information ready for him to look over and work with. Walk through the program treatment. Describe what you want to convey, what you want the program to accomplish, and how you want the audience to feel about it. Pass along any other ideas noted during the first meeting.

Point out any essential features or program highlights. Make the writer aware of special words or phrases your company uses. Talk about your organization's philosophy. And underline any no-no's like mentioning the competition by name or dating the material.

When you tell a writer that you want a first draft in one week, make it clear that you don't mean you want to see a rough view of how she may ultimately approach the subject. A first draft must be as close to final copy as possible. Any changes between the first and final script should be minor.

HOW MANY ACTORS WILL YOU NEED?

Here's a guide for determining how many people you may need for specific types of programs:

New product introduction

- 1 on-camera or voiceover talent
- 1 on-camera or voiceover talent with 2–3 actors
- 2–3 actors

News program

- 1 or 2 on-camera anchors

Informational

- 1 on-camera or voiceover talent

Motivational

- 1 on-camera or voiceover talent

Training

- 1 on-camera or voiceover talent
- 1 or 2 on-camera or voiceover talent with 2–3 role players

As you can see, this can get quite elaborate. I can't recommend using more than four or five people your first time out. The more characters you have, the easier it is to distract your audience, and the more it's going to cost you. You want to keep your program as simple as possible. The scriptwriter knows this and will offer suggestions based on his experience.

HOW WILL THE ACTORS BE USED?

Given the type of program you want to produce, the scriptwriter will help you decide whether the talent will appear on-camera or act in a voiceover capacity. Each has its own advantages and disadvantages.

On-camera talent advantages:

- Establishes a face with a voice
- Adds authority to the subject
- Adds motion to the script
- Breaks up visual elements
- Conveys intimacy with the audience

Disadvantages:

- Choice may run counter to company image
- On-camera shoots can last for days
- Actor becomes a "talking head"
- Delivery may not ring true
- Appearance may not enhance visual elements

Voiceover talent advantages:

- Voice is easy to manipulate and edit
- Allows for more than one version of the script
- Avoids visual distractions
- Moods and textures are easier to convey

Disadvantages:

- Loss of visual identification
- Disembodied voice may lack impact
- Regional dialect may seem out of place

SIGNING A CONTRACT

Figure 6.2 is a sample scriptwriting contract. As you can see, it spells out an agreed-upon fee for the work to be done along with delivery dates for the first draft and final script. The scriptwriter will either bring along a contract for the two of you to review and sign, or he may fax it to you later when he has had a chance to fill in the appropriate information.

Notice that the contract also covers writing expenses, project delays, and how the script will be submitted. Expenses should be minimal, especially if you're providing all the necessary information, but ask what else besides messenger fees and long-distance phone calls qualify as expenses. The section on project delays merely protects the writer from being on an indef-

(Date)

(Client Name)

Dear (Client):

I am looking forward to working with you on (Project Name).

Fee: The fee on which we agreed is $X,XXX, which covers submission of the first draft, revisions, and the final script.

Deadlines: I'll submit the first draft to you by (Date), with the final script by (Date).

Expenses: I'll invoice you for any messenger fees, or long-distance phone calls. I'll bill these charges separately and document them with an invoice from my vendors.

Delays: If the project is delayed or put on hold for more than 30 days, I'll bill all work to date.

Submission: I will send you hard copies of the script by fax or messenger, whichever you prefer. I can also furnish the script on disk, in either WordPerfect or as an ASCII file, or modem the electronic file to you.

Billing: I will invoice the project in two parts, with the first part billable on your acceptance of this agreement, and the balance due on submission of the final script. My terms are net and payable within 30 days of the invoice date.

Let me know if you have any questions regarding this agreement. If not, please sign below and return it to me by fax.

Thanks again, (Client). I look forward to our work together.

(CLIENT SIGNATURE)   (SCRIPTWRITER SIGNATURE)
(DATE)   (DATE)

Figure 6.2   Sample Scriptwriter Contract

inite, non-paid retainer in the event that someone changes her mind about the project and decides it can wait, and submission alternatives provide flexibility. If a scriptwriter offers a computer disk version of the program as part of his services, take it.

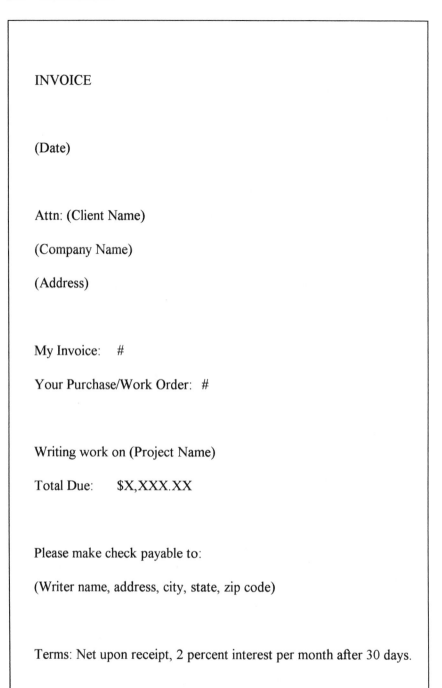

Figure 6.3 Sample Scriptwriting Invoice

The last section of the contract deals with how the work will be paid for. Depending on the scriptwriter you hire, there are several options that apply:

1. 1/3 on contract signing—1/3 after submission of first draft—1/3 after submission of final script
2. 1/2 on contract signing—1/2 after submission of final script
3. Full payment after submission of final script

From the producer's standpoint, the third option is ideal. There's less paperwork, you pay for the service in one lump sum, and it ensures delivery. From the scriptwriter's point of view, however, the first two options are more advantageous, not because they're greedy and want their money right away, but because they want to ensure that at least part of their time will be reimbursed should the project be suddenly discontinued. There's another reason. Ask scriptwriters about their most frustrating experiences, and they'll tell you about the company that took six months to pay them. Like any business, freelance scriptwriters have their own bills to pay.

Figure 6.3 is a sample invoice. Once you discuss and agree to the scriptwriter's fee and billing procedure, the invoice you receive should be straightforward and include any attachments covering miscellaneous expenses. If you have any questions relating to such items as long-distance calls, ask to see an itemized bill.

SCRIPT FORMATS

When you receive the first draft of your script, the look will be unfamiliar to you. It won't be like reading a book, in which you visualize a scene as you read it, nor will it read like a magazine or newspaper article. Video scripts break information down into images and words. By assigning specific images to specific words, the director, talent, and editor will know exactly what is to be said and what is to be done at specific moments.

There are three basic script layouts, each with its own advantages and disadvantages. The managers and executives who read your scripts will expect to see a familiar layout from show to show, so whatever style your scriptwriter employs, try to be consistent.

The Two-Column Script (Figure 6.4)

The most common format, the two-column script has a video column on the left and an audio column on the right. Audio text is double-spaced; video text is single-spaced. Both sides incorporate upper- and lowercase letters. The format is easy to read, leaves room in the margins for revisions, and is visually clean.

-VIDEO-	-AUDIO-
Narrator Appears on-camera.	This is the audio portion of the script.
Narrator takes the reader on a tour of the script.	Note that there is plenty of space in the margins for ideas and corrections.
Narrator tries to read large type but gets a headache.	Text can be entered in ALL CAPS, BUT IT CAN BE DIFFICULT TO READ IF YOUR SCRIPT IS VERY LONG.
Narrator is relaxed and able to read the audio portion just fine.	It's best to stay with upper and lowercase letters. Keep your paragraphs short and to the point.

Figure 6.4   Sample Two-Column Script

Some scriptwriters prefer the audio portion to be set in uppercase letters, but this method is tiring for the eyes, especially if the script is long. Your talent will have a difficult time reading a script if it is presented this way.

The most common complaint about this format is that the stark separation of words and images doesn't present a clear flow of ideas because the reader must constantly shift back and forth across the page from image to words and back again. Keep this in mind when submitting scripts for approval. Leave plenty of reading time, because the experience may be awkward at first. After you read through a few scripts, the format becomes easier to follow.

VIDEO

THE NARRATOR APPEARS ON-CAMERA.

AUDIO

This is the audio portion of the script

VIDEO

NARRATOR TAKES THE READER ON A TOUR OF THE SCRIPT.

AUDIO

Notice how this particular format alternates sight and sound as we might order the scene in our mind.

VIDEO

NARRATOR POINTS TO THE VIDEO LINES.

AUDIO

Unlike the two-column example, this format can be broken up by placing video text IN CAPS.

Figure 6.5   Sample Wide-Column Script

The Wide-Column Script (Figure 6.5)

This format comes closest to the way we visualize and describe the world around us; that is, in a progression of images and the words to explain them.

Notice how the words and images follow one another. If you were reading this script for the first time, you would find its information easy to grasp. Notice that the video portion of the script is set in caps while the audio portion uses upper- and lowercase letters. This helps break up an otherwise monotonous format, and makes the video portion of the program easier to locate for scene breakdowns.

The problem with this format is that it leaves no room for comments and changes. In fact, it necessitates using separate sheets of paper for notes.

FADE IN TO:

1 INT. PLUSH OFFICE -- EARLY EVENING

NARRATOR is sitting at a desk reading over a script. It is a long script, and the clock on the wall reads 6 p.m.

MEDIUM SHOT

NARRATOR
Boy, this script sure is taking forever to read.
Whoever wrote this should have their word
processor confiscated.

(looks up at the audience)

Oh, hi there! This is what a screenplay looks like. It
has a unique format, with scene descriptions, camera
positions, dialogue, and actions as separate entries.

2   CLOSE SHOT

NARRATOR picks up several pages of script from the desktop and waves it in the air.

NARRATOR
Screenplays are fun to write, but unless you have a
computer program that can automate the exact
position of all these elements, you'll spend most of
your time measuring margins.

Figure 6.6 Sample Screenplay Script

The Screenplay Script (Figure 6.6)

This format is rarely used in video, but you'll occasionally run across it. Like the wide-column format, the screenplay style flows down the page from image to words and back again, only now the directions and words are centered on the page with lots of room in the margins for changes.

The disadvantage to using this format is really a matter of inconvenience. Unless the scriptwriter is using software that automates each element of the script, more time is spent setting the proper margins than on the program's content. This format is better left to the screenplay artist.

There are numerous variations on these formats, but the idea is the same: images and words working together.

PROGRAM FORMATS

Program content was discussed during your first planning meeting and you forged the ideas into a treatment. Now it's up to the scriptwriter to decide what program style and visual elements can be incorporated into the program. Each of the following approaches is useful under specific situations, and can be utilized in a variety of ways.

1. The talking head
2. The interview
3. The documentary
4. The how-to
5. The role play

1. *The talking head.*
The format looks just like it sounds. A narrator stands or sits in front of the camera and tells the audience about the subject. The talking head is simple to do and requires only the talent's ability to communicate effectively, but it's also the most deadly in terms of sustaining audience interest. This format should be used sparingly.

2. *The interview.*
Conducting interviews is an art form mastered by few professionals. Whether you stage an interview or gather spontaneous responses, this format adds credibility to any topic. Like the talking head, it can also be boring if interviews are strung one after the other.

(Questions must be phrased properly to ensure full-bodied responses from the participant. All too often, interviews quickly degenerate into a series of yes/no responses and will do little to illuminate your subject.)

3. *The documentary.*

Using location shots, interviews, and graphics, the documentary style provides a way of looking at a progression of ideas and actions, many times in an historical context.

This format doesn't always work in a corporate environment. Unlike the construction of a luxury liner or the development of a life-saving medical technique, the creation of a new financial planning product won't build a lot of interest or suspense no matter how excited its creators are. If the scriptwriter incorporates any documentary features into your video, they should be short and to the point.

4. *The how-to.*

This format physically demonstrates how something works, usually in a step-by-step fashion. For a new product introduction, this means listing product features, then showing how those features work. This format can also cover commission calculations, proper forms handling, and home office procedures.

5. *The role play.*

Role playing presents its own challenges as talent become sales reps, executives, clients, and employees who solve a problem. A new employee, for example, discovers that she can improve her efficiency and skills by taking advantage of a new computer course teaching the latest desktop publishing or word processing program.

These are the most common program formats, but certainly not the only ones. In addition, the scriptwriter may use more than one format to keep the program fresh, so don't be surprised if the script uses a talking head in one scene, then a role play, a how-to sequence, and then another talking head.

SCRIPTWRITING SOFTWARE

In the early days of video production, scripts were dutifully pounded out on typewriters. Errors were erased, x'd out, or covered up with correction fluid. Changes were a curse, especially if an addition or subtraction threw off page numbers. Retyping twenty pages of script was a chore to be avoided. No wonder writers fought so hard for their words.

Computers have changed the writing business. The screen has taken the place of paper, and electrons the place of ink. Need to move a paragraph to the end of the program? Just block it and move it. Need to add more dialogue? Don't worry, the text and page numbers will automatically adjust themselves.

Scriptwriters have benefited greatly from the technology. Not only are scripts visually cleaner and more polished, but production time has been reduced. Today's writers can work on several scripts simultaneously, manipulating their words through several rewrites until their clients are satisfied.

There may come a time, however, when you'll want to exercise greater control over your programs by writing scripts yourself. Appendix E lists some of the software available. Call or write for a demo disk and information.

SCRIPT DIRECTIONS

The first time you read through a script, some of the directions may seem foreign to you, prompting a quick call to the scriptwriter to find out what "POV: Zoom CS on Brochure" means. Save yourself some time by becoming familiar with the following terms.

FS: Full shot

WS: Wide shot

LS: Long shot

MLS: Medium long shot

MS: Medium shot

MCS: Medium close shot　(MCU—Medium Closeup—is also used)

CS: Close shot　(CU—Closeup—is also used)

TCS: Tight close shot　(TCU—Tight Closeup—is also used)

ECS: Extreme close shot　(ECU—Extreme Closeup—is also used)

POV: Point-of-view

OTS: Over-the-shoulder

Without getting too technical, a full shot shows performers in their entirety, a medium shot shows them from the waist up, and a close shot frames the subject from the shoulders up.

Point-of-view invites the reader to see the action through the eyes of the narrator or a character. An over-the-shoulder shot provides another perspective, such as a conversation when the camera shifts between two speakers in conversation.

Here are some other terms you should be familiar with:

Insert: A scene to be shot and added later in post-production.

VO: A voiceover.

OS: Out-of-shot. A person heard but not seen on camera.

Cut: An immediate jump from one scene to another.

Dissolve: The fading of one scene into another.

Wipe: The pushing of one scene offscreen by another.

Fade-in/Fade-out: An increase/decrease in image from/to black.

Pan: A horizontal camera move.

Tilt: A vertical camera move.

Zoom in/Zoom out: An increase or decrease in image size.

Freeze: A moving image held in place.

Now that you know something about script directions, have them removed from your first draft. Some scriptwriters have a tendency to "direct on paper" by throwing in every angle and camera movement they can think of. While this may look impressive, it's unnecessary. Let the director decide what movements and angles will work best to make the words come alive. Also, make sure that your script is not numbered by scene. When the house producer or director goes over the script with the crew, she will set scene numbers that will make it easier for her to keep track of what was shot in a studio and what was shot on location.

Most directors will ignore script directions unless something needs to be shot a particular way. The problem is not one of creative styles but of efficiency. Once the script is completed, the writer has nothing more to do with the project. It will only waste time if a production company has to track down the writer to figure out what he had in mind on page three of the script.

If you're satisfied with your choice in a scriptwriter, he'll take your treatment, information, ideas, and input from others and assimilate them into a well-paced, motivating script. He will be visually minded, be able to write in a short, easy-to-follow manner, and have an ear for the spoken word.

Scriptwriters don't often admit it—and those hiring them rarely say it—but the lines of communication must remain open at all times. You have to inform the writer if more information becomes available. The scriptwriter has to tell you if something is not clear, or if your logic in structuring the program is confusing. He must also explain why he cannot meet a deadline.

Too often, failure to talk leads to disappointment and frustration. One thought the other meant this date instead of that; the script is a day late and you can't reach the writer, etc. Then there's the obvious disaster of getting a script that's totally different from what you wanted. This shouldn't happen, but it does. You can either sit down with the writer and try to hammer out the problems, or you can pay him for his work and start again. The latter pushes everything else in your production schedule up and will cost more than your budget allows—all the more reason to be as clear and as thorough as you possibly can about your project.

With the scriptwriter hired and two weeks to go before the final script is due, you're now in the most critical period of your production schedule. Whatever you do during the next two weeks will eventually be reflected in the look of your program.

That look will be created by the production company.

AT THIS STAGE OF THE PRE-PRODUCTION PROCESS YOU SHOULD

- Analyze a scriptwriter's potential using the "SPT" check: samples, price, and time.
- Study sample scripts for clarity and the ability to convey key information.
- Meet with the scriptwriter to talk about his experience and your production needs, and to define your expectations and those of your company.
- Discuss payment and turnaround time, using your production calendar.
- Familiarize yourself with the various script and program formats, scriptwriting software, and script directions.
- Stay in touch with the scriptwriter to ensure that you get the script you want.

7

Finding and Working with a Production Company

Now you have to find a production house that suits your needs.

Production companies have very different orientations and philosophies. You will find many advertisements in a creative directory, and all may sound like they can get the job done, but be very careful!

Many production houses are geared specifically to large companies and corporations. Some have invested millions of dollars in high-tech equipment, technicians, and artists. Going to them for a one-camera, one-person studio shoot requiring few graphics is like shooting goldfish with a cannon. They could certainly do the job for you, but they'd much rather schedule a major client that has a taste for special effects and money to spend.

Your best bet lies with production services that cater to small-to-medium companies. They'll be more sensitive to your budget and will schedule talent, editing facilities, and duplication services for you. They are usually small operations and will be eager to have your business, especially if they have a shot at repeat business.

HOW TO FIND THE RIGHT PRODUCTION COMPANY

There are three basic types of production houses:

1. Companies with in-house facilities and full-service capabilities, from concept and scriptwriting to editing and duplication
2. Companies with basic in-house facilities such as a studio, but which contract out for scripting, editing, and duplication elsewhere
3. Companies that have no in-house facilities, preferring to hire out some or all production services on a per-job basis

The only certainty among these three types of houses is that the first will cost you well beyond your budget. These are companies that are used to blank checks. If you work for a small company or organization, the second and third choices will do the job nicely. They've invested in high-quality equipment. Some may not have a studio or editing facility, but they can subcontract. This is an area where shopping around can really make a difference.

There are differences, too, between the full-service producer and the independent producer, differences that can be the difference between a good show and a great show.

The full-service house producer has every conceivable resource right at her fingertips. Any question you raise or problem that develops during a production can be handled immediately. A solution is always brewing in the next room. If your house producer has a personal stake in guiding your program carefully through the production process, the experience can be very rewarding. It's a great way to experience every facet of the video industry without leaving the building.

Unfortunately, not all houses operate this way. Keep in mind that at any given time a production house will be involved in at least a dozen programs, and your producer may be involved in two or three of them. It's easy to get lost in the shuffle. Depending upon how important your account is, you may find less than exclusive service. Your program may seem like an assembly line job, and not a very good one, at that.

The independent producer, for the most part, has to work harder. Without a lot of competitive capital, smaller production companies place a greater emphasis on knowing where to get the best job done, which allows them much greater flexibility in terms of technology and artistic talent. They also have to keep up with their larger counterparts.

You will find that the independent producer wears many hats. He may also be a writer, cameraperson, director, or editor. This often stems from economic necessity, but you'll also find that these producers like taking on additional responsibilities. They feel closer to their work when they can take a hands-on approach. Many producers are ex-television and feature film artisans, which adds depth to their understanding of the industry.

Smaller production companies have their limitations. A couple of cameras and a tape deck do not a production company make. If your producer has trouble visualizing a script, or seems hesitant to try something new, it's a pretty good sign that he doesn't have much experience. Another drawback is in range of programming. A company may stay within specific genres— corporate training programs, for example. The reason is that it simply lacks the resources offered by the bigger houses, and has kept its range limited to accommodate the more popular needs of the marketplace. It has very little to do with talent.

People are often surprised at the complexity and sophistication of the video industry. To most, a studio is just that, an empty room with a camera and a couple of walls that frame the set. The director sits in a chair next to the camera, the talent have their lines memorized, and the client is nowhere to be seen.

Times have changed. Here are some of the in-house features provided by a few full-service production houses in the Chicago area:

- Fully operational kitchens, including microwave ovens and deep freezers
- Private client offices
- Satellite and microwave feeds and receivers
- Exercise room
- Private aircraft for shuttling clients on location
- Underwater and aerial equipment and photography
- Translation services
- Wood, metal, and electric shops
- Screening rooms, makeup rooms, and dressing rooms with showers
- Video monitors in every room, so you can watch what's happening from anywhere on the premises

If you're looking for something a bit out of the ordinary, there are also houses that will cheerfully cater to special needs. These include forensic reconstruction, scientific visualization, and even architecture and engineering. Take your pick.

So when you're looking around for a house to produce your video, remember that there is a company to realize your every wish and whim, provided you have the money to pay for it.

WHAT TO LOOK FOR IN A PRODUCTION COMPANY

All production houses, regardless of size and technological sophistication, share the same type of clientele, namely business.

As you did with the scriptwriter—and will do later on with the talent—you do need to find a production house that has produced a program similar to yours before, preferably within your line of business. Two documentary filmmakers who are branching out into industrial video are not going to cut it. This is no time to experiment.

Figure 7.1 is a fairly typical entry in a creative directory. As we discussed briefly in Chapter 2, a production ad contains an address, phone number, and key production personnel.

HOLLYWOOD IN THE STICKS PRODUCTIONS   555-5555

                                                    Fax 555-5555

One Big Building/Suite 10000/Downtown

AWARD-WINNING SERVICE AT AFFORDABLE PRICES

Bill U. Later - President/Executive Producer

John E. Cash - Director/Cameraman

Tessie Tura   - Art Director

J. Jack Flash - Writer/Sales Representative

A FULL-SERVICE production facility featuring the latest in high-tech innovation.

SPECIALIZING IN small to medium sized companies and corporations and

community groups. Will do training programs and commercial work in addition to

commercials and television.

FEATURING the new Abracadabra SX-9000 computer enhanced video editing

system with multitrack audio capabilities and special effects.

STUDIO dimensions include a complete 50' x 40' soundstage and smaller studios

for all production and post-production needs.

CLIENTS include Mom & Pop Bicycle Repair, Ed's Summer Ranch, and the

Downtown Chamber of Commerce.

CALL FOR OUR LATEST DEMO REEL OR STOP BY FOR A TOUR.

Figure 7.1 Sample Production Company Ad

As you read through the ad copy, note how the company chose to present itself. Some companies are very obvious about their desire to work with big budgets; for example, if the copy says the company has won more than a dozen Emmys or Clios, chances are that the staff won't be interested in your project even though they claim to do corporate videos.

Other companies prefer to let their in-house facilities and equipment do the talking. When the copy refers to sound stage dimensions, Abekas A57s with SuperWarp, digital disc recorders, and interactive video capabilities, you're in over your head, at least for the moment.

Still others refer to some of their clients, big-name companies whose commercials you see on TV. This provides a good clue that the ad is speaking to other big-name companies who are shopping around for someone to put together their latest campaign. The same goes for people who say that they've been in the business for 40 years and have six offices throughout the country.

If you get the feeling that the video community is in business to satisfy the mega-budget needs of multinational corporations, you're right. Video is very big business. But that doesn't mean you can't find someone to take on your project.

As you read through a directory, write down those candidates that offer a middle-of-the-road approach to the industry. These ads will simply state that they produce audiovisual and video programs for business applications and offer a range of production services.

If you have established a network with other companies in your industry, call your contacts, read off your list of possible producers, and ask for a referral. Companies that have learned video production through trial and error will help you avoid mistakes with a wealth of tips. They can also point out which companies are good for certain types of shows, such as news or training programs, and which companies to stay away from.

Call at least three companies and ask them to send you the following:

1. Demo reel
2. Client list
3. Rate sheet
4. List of services

1. *Demo reel*
In many ways demo reels provide a good indication of what you can expect from a company, but they can also be slick presentations totally lacking in substance.

Demo reels last no more than five minutes and are arranged in a highlight format. The best scene from each program is given fifteen or twenty seconds of time, then on to the next scene. Some companies will bombard you with fast-moving snippets and equally fast electronic music. In other words, there are no set presentation rules.

You can pick up a lot of information from a demo reel:

Quality. If the picture is clear and sharp and the sound is crisp, the company is using high-quality equipment and tape. You definitely want this.

Talent. Do the people look natural? Do you believe they are who they say they are? If the production company arranges talent, this shows that it has a good feel for business needs.

Visuals. How well did a company visualize the spoken word? Even in a twenty-second clip, you can tell how well a story is told. After all, the purpose of a demo reel is to sell you on a company's abilities.

2. *Client list*

Requesting a client list is a perfectly natural part of the process. Far from being suspicious of a company's claims, any reputable production house will gladly tell you how much it was able to do for your neighbors, especially those in your industry. It's a matter of pride, like wearing an achievement badge.

If you follow up with any of the past clients, be sure to identify yourself and ask how the producer and/or director was to work with.

3. *Rate sheet*

Since the production end of the video is the one that will make up the greater part of your budget, make no mistake about setting the table now. A rate sheet provides clues as to what is negotiable and what isn't.

For instance, tape stock and talent fees are not up for discussion. Editing time is negotiable unless the production company has to rent an editing suite instead of using an in-house facility. Based on the complexity of the script—which determines the number of people needed to shoot it—and the fact that you're a first-time client, the house producer may reduce some charges. That's something you'll have to discuss when you bring her in to talk about your project.

4. *List of services*

This last item is very important. Aside from hiring a company to shoot the script, you want someone who will help arrange talent, editing time, and duplication. The less time you must spend to arrange these on your own, the more you'll be able to spend on other elements of the production. Later on you can arrange these services separately.

MEETING WITH A PRODUCTION COMPANY

Once again, review all submitted material, choose the most promising company, and set up a meeting with staff members.

Your discussions should be similar to the one you had with the scriptwriter. Let them talk about themselves first. They'll want to anyway since they're going to try and sell you on their abilities and accomplishments. Watch the demo reel with them and ask what went into each of the segments. What problems did they encounter when making these programs, and how did they solve them? What type of camera and other equipment did they use?

While selling you on themselves, they will also try to sell you on their latest investments, like a sophisticated paintbox or animation package. It sounds great, but never lose sight of your needs. Don't be lulled into creating a more elaborate production than is necessary. All you need for now is one camera and a tape deck, a microphone, and tape stock. After you receive the first draft of the script and give a copy to the house producer, you can talk about enhancing the program with visual effects.

Provide a copy of the treatment and all the program information you have. Explain what you want. Break down the production into basic needs.

The production company staff will have some questions for you. The production schedule will give them dates to work with, but they will want to know if you want them to hire the talent, arrange editing time, etc. They will also want to know what graphics they will have to create, whether computer-generated or through traditional artwork. The treatment should answer any other questions.

IS THE PRODUCTION COMPANY INSURED?

The last thing you want to think about when producing a video is the possibility that someone might be injured during the course of the shoot or that property will be damaged. However, accidents will happen and, in a litigation-happy society, you can't afford to be unprotected.

The production company you hire must have insurance and be able to prove it. This is not a problem you'll encounter with medium- and larger-sized production houses that have their own crews and equipment, but if you choose to work with a two- or three-person company that relies on a lot of sub-contracting, asking about their insurance coverage is absolutely essential. Without it, you and your company will be totally liable for anything that happens on the set or on location.

Liability is something all legitimate production companies are concerned about. A producer friend of mine told me a story that underscores this point. His company was hired by a corporation to provide a crew and cameras for a location shoot. This corporation also hired separate companies to provide lights, props, and other equipment. During the location setup, someone fell off a scaffolding and incurred multiple injuries. Who did the injured party sue? Everyone, including my friend. He eventually had his name dropped from the suit, since his company's involvement in the shoot had nothing to do with the circumstances surrounding the injury, but it cost him a considerable amount of time and money to do so.

There's no reason to expect that your production will experience the same fate. In all the years I've been involved in video production I've never seen anyone injured or any property damaged. A well-planned production minimizes risks, and a professional production crew constantly has safety in mind. If you need to shoot in a potentially hazardous place, make sure the house producer knows about it ahead of time and take her there to assess what needs to be done or provided to do the job right.

WHAT TO LOOK FOR IN A PRODUCTION BID

When your meeting is concluded, the house producer will put a bid together showing you how much the production company will charge given the information you provided at the meeting. A sample bid might include something like this:

Studio and Location Shooting

Full-day, 2-person production crew at $1200/day for three days:
($3,600 JVC 3CCD camera, Sony VO-8800 portable deck, Lowell 4K lighting kit, Shure SM-58 microphone, Lectrosonics wireless system, Shure M-267 field mixer)

Talent: 2 on-camera talent for 3 days at $1,000/day/person: $6,000

Editing: 2 days editing at $300/hour for 16 hours: $4,800

Tape stock: $300

Duplication: 100 program copies at $10/copy with labels: $1,000

Total cost: $15,700

There will be a one- or two-day time lag in receiving a bid because many production companies need to call editors and duplicators to check on their prices and availability. Read the bid carefully. Did they cover everything you talked about?

Here are some things to look out for when reviewing a bid:

Hidden charges. If you don't see equipment rentals, travel expenses, parking, or phone calls included in the bid, call and ask if they're included in the package. If not, have the company submit a list of any other estimated costs. Some companies will deliberately lowball their bids just to get your business, then hit you with a much higher final bill after their work is done.

Bait-and-switch. I'm sorry to say that not everyone in the video business has your best interests at heart. The bid may say they'll use the latest camera model to shoot your program, but then they'll use an older model and charge you a higher price. That's why it's important to ask what type of camera they used to shoot the programs you saw in their demo reel. If you like the look, get a commitment to use the same camera, and hold them to it.

Broadcast quality. Beware these words. "Broadcast quality" means about the same as saying a record player produces stereo sound. What constitutes broadcast quality? No, it's not what you see when you turn on the evening news; in fact it doesn't have anything to do with picture quality at all. To date, no one has been able to establish what this phrase really means. The Federal Communications Commission (FCC) only defines acceptable broadcast signals in terms of pulse durations and levels. As long as the equipment used in the making of your program meets the minimum requirements, it passes the FCC test. How your program will look is another matter. If you see the words "broadcast quality" in a bid without any indication as to what equipment the production company intends to use, ask for specifics and a video sample of what that equipment can do.

THE PRE-PRODUCTION MEETING

When you hire a production company, the staff will want to set up a pre-production meeting. The treatment has already allowed for this in the schedule; it falls one day after the delivery of the first draft of the script.

The production company will bring along a dozen or so pictures of possible talent, and may bring audio demo reels so you can hear them, as matching a face to a voice helps in the selection process. We'll cover talent in the next chapter, but for now be aware that the production company will check on the availability of any chosen talent and will arrange to have them come in and read for you in person if you need to get managerial approvals.

Some of the other things you'll discuss during pre-production include:

1. Studio and location taping
2. Editing
3. Program duplication
4. Tape labels
5. Additional services

1. *Studio and location taping*
What you do on the set or on location is important if you want to establish any credibility with your audience.

If you're shooting on location, say, in the home of a prospective client, make sure the home that is used falls within the demographics and economics of your company's clientele. One company I worked for catered to a very definite income range. If you shoot a scene in a mansion, and your clientele is middle working class, your audience is going to write you off and laugh at your ignorance. The same holds true for a studio shoot. If you're going to use an office setting and your talent is going to portray a sales rep, make sure the set looks like an actual sales office. Nothing is more distracting in a video than a fake set.

When the production company receives a copy of the script, the house producer will be able to tell how much time will be needed for studio and location taping. Here's where production holes come into play. Based on the production schedule we set up in Chapter 3, we left two days for location taping and two days for studio taping, a total of four days. After reviewing the script, the house producer decides that most of the script can be done in the studio in an eight-hour day, with only a couple of scenes needed on location. Four days are now reduced to two. This will make a considerable difference in your final bill, as the bid originally projected four days' worth of work. Not every script will result in such a reduction, but at least your schedule allows for extra days if they are needed, and extra time for your regular job duties if they're not.

Make note of what you're expected to provide for these shoots. A new product introduction will require that you bring along the appropriate sales or prospecting kits, a training video, and any textbooks, workbooks, or software packages. Whatever the house producer asks you to bring along, get it together right away. Don't wait until the day before a shoot to do it.

2. *Editing*

Should you only need two days for studio and location taping, you can move up the editing dates, which will free up even more time in your schedule. The only thing the production company has to do is confirm the days and times.

Choosing the right editing facility—if the production company doesn't have its own—depends on the complexities of the script. Modest budgets like yours won't need Star Wars–type special effects, so an equally modest post-production facility will do.

3. *Program duplication*

How many copies of the program will you need? Duplication prices vary from service to service, but the more copies you order, the less you'll pay per tape. Production companies don't usually shop around. They know who does the best work, so trust their choice.

4. *Tape labels*

Most people don't think of this until it's too late, but designing personalized company tape labels adds yet another note of detail to your shows. They look distinctive when placed side by side on a shelf, and they encourage company pride.

The process of creating personalized labels involves submitting camera-ready art to your house producer. The question you must answer is: Do you want your company's title and logo on the outside box, the spine, the tape, or all three?

Once you've answered that question, your next consideration will be coordinating the proper logo color.

We take the colors we see and describe for granted, but there's an exact cataloguing system that makes sure that when you say "sky blue," everyone knows what you're talking about.

Graphic artists rely upon the Pantone Matching System—or PMS—to establish consistency. This is a universally accepted form of color denomination; your logo color has a specific PMS number. Whether you use a duplication house in Arizona or Maine, mentioning the PMS number immediately establishes the proper color.

If you have a graphic arts department in your company, ask someone there for the number. If not, whoever printed your company logo on letterhead and other company items will be able to tell you. If all else fails, the duplicator can take the logo and do the matching.

What happens next is quite simple. The duplicator takes your logo, and plates are made. Whenever you need labels, blanks are run through a machine with the proper PMS color and your logo appears, flawlessly and professionally.

The production company can arrange to have labels made for you. The first time around it will take about a month to six weeks to have the plates made and the labels run off, depending on your needs. If you're going to do this, set it up as early as possible.

5. *Additional services*

What else can a production company do for you?

Think about not only your primary audience but any potential markets for your program. Let's say you're producing an instructional video aimed at teaching people how to use an automated teller machine. You want to reach as many people as possible, don't you? Then think about having your program captioned or translated into other languages.

According to the Americans with Disabilities Act (ADA), all businesses and governments must make their services available and accessible to those with disabilities. Captioning your video program for the deaf and hard-of-hearing can help you reach a wider audience. And if your company is expanding its clientele to service non-English-speaking communities, having your script translated can make a world of difference.

The production company you hire may not have these services readily available, but it can send your master tape out to other companies to have them done. Be sure to get all applicable costs and turnaround times before you make a decision.

THE FINAL BILL: A CAUTIONARY TALE

When you receive the final bill for your production, compare the charges listed in the invoice with the services listed in the bid you agreed to. Nine and three-quarter times out of ten they should match up. It's that last quarter you have to watch out for.

Most of the videos I produced for a company were pretty evenly spread out over the course of the year, but at one point we found ourselves quite busy. I was already involved in two separate video projects, so my manager took on a third and hired a husband-and-wife production team to shoot his script. Even though the manager was not able to attend the studio and location tapings, he worked closely with the couple on the show's visual look, they gave him what he wanted, and the program looked great.

While out of town for a conference, my manager called and asked me to take care of the invoice on his project when it came in. When I got the bill, I read through the charges and could not believe what I was seeing. Aside from charging us for their production services, which were what we expected, the couple also charged us a separate fee for using the wife as talent, for using their home as a location, and for long-distance calls made during the location day. These charges were buried in the invoice, added into a paragraph here and a line there.

These charges were outrageously high. The next time my manager called in, I asked him if he had had any discussions about using the wife as talent. I asked if he had agreed to using the couple's home for a location, and if so did they discuss at what cost. Then I asked what long-distance calls the couple could possibly have made that pertained to the project. My manager was stumped on all counts and furious at being taken advantage of. The bottom line was that we were charged an extra $5,000 for these questionable services, and in the end we had the charges removed from the invoice and never worked with the couple again.

This kind of incident happened only once in my career, but it serves as a good reminder to others. Know what you're paying for. Read your invoice thoroughly. And question anything you didn't discuss or agree to.

Over the course of the production you'll be working very closely with your house producer, asking and answering questions, confirming dates, and making adjustments to your production plans. If your producer asks you to come visit her facilities or join her for a day on another shoot, do so. This will give you a better idea of what to expect from her and the production process.

With your production and post-production dates now set, let's talk about talent.

AT THIS STAGE OF THE PRE-PRODUCTION PROCESS YOU SHOULD

- Consider the three types of production houses available to you, and understand their abilities and limitations.
- Use your resources and contacts to locate at least three production companies.
- Request demo reels, rate sheets, client lists, and information on other production services to help you choose the most promising production house.
- Set up a pre-production meeting to review and discuss your project, and set dates for taping and editing based on your production calendar.
- Explore the possibility of having your program captioned or translated to reach a wider audience.
- Make sure any invoice for services you receive matches the production bid you agreed to.

8

Talent

There are people out there who tell us what to do. They tell us what to wear, what to eat, how to take care of ourselves, how we should live, and constantly remind us that we are consumers, that we believe in certain values, and that consumers love to buy things.

No, Big Brother hasn't come to town to set up shop, but these forceful pronouncements are just as persuasive. They dominate television and radio, magazines and newspapers, and just about every other form of communication we come into contact with on a daily basis. The people who tell us what to do are professional talent. If you have something to sell, they will help you sell it. It makes no difference whether it's an idea or a product.

The talent business is so big and far-reaching that it often takes on mythic proportions in the way it shapes our thoughts and actions. If advertising agencies provide the engines that make our economy run, then talent provide the power. And you're about to plug into it.

WHO ARE THESE PEOPLE, ANYWAY?

There are three unions involved in the talent business. There is the Screen Actors Guild (SAG), which handles primarily film, television, and commercial jobs; the American Federation of Television and Radio Artists (AFTRA), which deals with video and voiceover work; and the Actors' Equity Association (AEA), which deals with theater actors and actresses. The talent you choose may belong to one or all three unions.

These unions are licensed by the Department of Labor and as such are highly regulated. When you deal with a talent agency that has a union affiliation, you can be sure that it stands by its people and has taken care to represent only the finest talent. But that doesn't mean you have to use an agency that is exclusively union. Many agencies represent non-union talent that can provide equally effective service.

The unions exist for the profitable use of talent. They make sure their people are paid, provide retirement and medical benefits, and offer legal assistance. They also exist for you. They want your production to look and sound its best, and they've got the right people for the job. Once you've established a rapport with a local talent agency or two, you're never more than a phone call away from help.

You're going to need some kind of assistance, because your choice of talent will decide whether or not your audience believes in you. For obvious reasons, then, your choice should reflect your company's values, philosophy, social makeup, and personality.

- If your audience is composed of career sales reps, don't use talent that "talks down" to them.
- Don't use younger talent unless your group is predominately young. This type of talent will not convey the proper sense of authority to an older audience.
- If your audience is male, don't use a female; if your audience is female, don't use a male.

This last point has more to do with credibility than anything else. Men are more apt to listen and respond to another man, and the same goes for women. They convey the needs, desires, and drives of their respective sexes much better. Imagine how well a man would go over talking about sexual harassment in the workplace, or how well a woman would go over talking about male pattern baldness.

CHOOSING TALENT

When you meet with your house producer to go over the first draft of the script, she should bring along at least a dozen photos of men and women she thinks most closely match the content and purpose of your program. Some producers will even bring along a portable video player or cassette player so you can see and hear the talent perform in a variety of programs.

This is a good time to get those granting approvals together to review your candidates. Expect to hear a variety of reasons why one talent should be used over another, all having to do with gut reactions and visual perceptions. Managers should get a positive first impression of anyone chosen to represent your company, but do remind them that a voice is just as important as a face, and if necessary play the demo tapes and reels over and over until a final decision is made.

If you're using more than one talent in your program, keep these tips in mind:

- Avoid the "white male syndrome." Give your program a solid mix of genders and races to reflect the makeup of your company, clientele, or audience.
- Talent come in all shapes and sizes. Not everyone in your show has to look like a celebrity or an international supermodel.
- Look and listen for distinctive features. A winning, confident smile works wonders on an audience, just as a casual or dramatic inflection at just the right moment adds extra punch to a script.

After you've made your choice, decide on one or two backups, since the house producer will have to check on the talent's availability. Since your production dates are tentatively set, the agency rep will hold some dates for you.

HIRING TALENT ON YOUR OWN

If you contact an agency directly, explain what you're looking for and what your program is about. The rep in charge of scheduling can offer much in the way of assistance by suggesting a number of people to fit your needs.

Demo reels are provided free and come in either video or audio cassette formats. You can also get a black-and-white headshot of the talent to help match a voice with a face. On the back of every photo is a list of some of the programs the artist has done and the companies he's worked with. Figure 8.1 is an example of what a talent resumé looks like.

If you have access to a large enough room with good lighting and can get a decent video camera—even a camcorder—you can also schedule talent to come in for a personal reading. This service is provided free by the agency and will be set up for you. All you need to provide is a script for them to read. In this case, you can use the first draft of the script.

If you're not sure about the cost of an agency's talent, ask. The rep will give you a breakdown as to how much you'll be paying for their time, and what percentage of their fee is applied to agency commissions and benefits. This will add to your general knowledge of the talent industry and give you something to explain if management ever asks why talent costs so much.

Using Non-Union Talent

If you want to explore other routes, you may find less expensive talent without sacrificing quality. They may not come from an agency, but they can still be effective.

The best source is to check with your community theater company, a great wealth of talent just waiting to be tapped. On more than one occasion I used two very talented people from just such a group. Both were retired

---

JOE SPOKESMAN

SAG-AFTRA-AEA

The Talent Agency

555-5555

HEIGHT: 6'5" **WEIGHT**: 210 **EYES**: Brown **HAIR**: Brown

TELEVISION/FILM:	"Aliens from the Deep"	Big Pictures
	"Beyond the Stars"	PBS Series
	"Have You Seen Me?"	MegaShow
VOICE WORK:	"Brand X Coffees"	Beans R' Us
	"Home Repair"	Wood Helpers
	"Sky Driver"	Luxury Autos
CORPORATE:	Training Programs	Giant Corp.
	News Shows	Company X
THEATER:	Man of Toledo	D-Theater
SPECIALTIES:	Spanish and Russian languages, Fencing, Nuclear Physics, Pyrotechnics	

Figure 8.1   Sample Talent Resumé

ex-agency people who had more than thirty years of experience doing local TV and radio. Even though they no longer openly advertised their services, they were more than willing to get in front of the camera or into a recording booth to stay in practice. They also charged considerably less than a union agency.

Another alternative is to use company employees as talent, although you should exercise this option only under special circumstances.

Department employees work best as background for location scenes that demonstrate home office procedures or to show how one area of the company works with another. This strengthens company involvement in the process and makes people feel they're playing an important role in their company's success. Even when used as voiceover talent, an employee's personal recollection or opinion can add great depth to any message.

On the other hand, refrain from using employees as on-camera talent. Chances are they've never been in front of a camera before and will most likely act stiff and uncertain, unable to deliver their lines in a convincing manner. There are exceptions, but you won't encounter them often.

You will, sooner or later, run across a manager or executive who insists that he and only he can sell this or motivate that. There are times when you'll want to use him—and you should certainly encourage his involvement—but he should be saved for the really important message. In the meantime, let the professional talent handle the rest.

Protect Yourself

Figure 8.2 is a sample release form. If you go out on your own and hire someone from a theater company or any other non-agency source, it's best to protect yourself and your company's interests.

Note that the release lists the date, program name, talent name, and price for services. As you read on you'll find a statement to the effect that once the payment is made, the talent has no further claim to the program. That is, the talent cannot come back later and demand more money if the program is duplicated and sent out to hundreds of sales offices. This also applies to photographs and slides and their use in print and audiovisual programs.

Work with your company's legal department to draft a release form. It should be simple and direct, leaving no doubt that the company has full use of the hired talent.

ON THE SET

Your responsibilities do not end with the hiring of talent. In other words, the narrator will not instinctively know how you want the script to be presented. He will count on you for direction.

In return, there will be times when the narrator will know more of what you want than you do and will make suggestions. Listen to what he's saying. Sometimes a turn of a phrase or a shift in emphasis can turn a simple statement into a profound declaration.

TALENT RELEASE FORM

DATE:

COMPANY:

TALENT NAME:

ADDRESS:

PHONE:

PAYMENT:

PROGRAM NAME:

I hereby authorize XYZ Company unlimited use of my voice and visual appearance and waive all rights for their use. In addition, the XYZ Company may reproduce and distribute the aforementioned program without prior notification and additional payment of same to me.

TALENT SIGNATURE:_____

DATE:_____

Figure 8.2   Sample Release Form

Some of the areas you'll have to work with talent on include:

- Pronunciation of the names of products, people, and places
- An understanding of how a product, service, or technique works
- An understanding of the audience

Talent pride themselves on being able to pronounce difficult technical and scientific words. You won't be able to trip them up very often, but go over key words with them just to be sure.

We often take the voices we hear and the people we see on radio and TV for granted. It all looks so easy. The reality of the situation is that voice work is very hard and very demanding. The men and women you see and hear may train for years before they're ready. Demo tapes have to be written, recorded, and duplicated, with boxes (mailing containers with the talent's picture and agency affiliation on them) specially tailored to the individual. Photos have to be taken and mass-produced. Resumés have to be created. Answering services have to be set up. And once that's done, they have to constantly keep their names, faces, and voices in front of people. This is not a business for the hesitant.

By the time you finish your first pre-production meeting, the first draft of the script is done and the production company is readying itself for the shoot. Up until now you've been dealing with various services, seeing the production in terms of bits and pieces. In the next chapter, we'll look at the script and make it real.

AT THIS STAGE OF THE PRE-PRODUCTION PROCESS YOU SHOULD

- Determine which qualities your talent should possess to best fulfill the needs of your video.
- Contact a local talent agency for demo reels, photos, and talent rates. If the production company arranges talent, have the producer bring along photos and demo reels to the pre-production meeting.
- Schedule time with company managers to choose your talent.
- Consider using local theater company talent for future productions.
- Draft a talent release form if you choose non-agency talent.
- Think about key words and phrases you may want to discuss with the talent while on the set.

9

Assembling Visual Elements

Take a breath for a moment, step back, and review everything that has happened so far:

- The scriptwriter submitted a first draft, a well-written and well-paced narrative with one on-camera or voiceover narrator, one or two location scenes, and plenty of opportunities to highlight and explain program points. With minor revisions, the text has been approved and sent back to the writer for a final script.
- The house producer, working from your treatment, production schedule, and script, has confirmed dates, times, and places for production and editing. In addition, she has hired the talent you want and contacted the duplicator to get prices and a delivery schedule should you need copies of the program.

Okay, so everything seems to be rolling along just fine. The rush is over; now you have some time before the shoot to relax and let the production run itself. Not quite. Unfortunately, any lack of attention to detail at this point will spell the creative end of the finished product. Your work has just begun.

First-time producers often assume that the production company is solely responsible for putting together the video's visual elements. After all, the talent has been lined up, there will be a day or two of location shooting, and the studio will put together a great set—what more could you possibly need?

A lot more. Making an ordinary video extraordinary is your responsibility. The following section offers some suggestions. Some of these ideas you can carry out on your own, or you can have your house producer follow up on them for you.

SIXTEEN WAYS TO ADD VISUAL POWER TO YOUR SCRIPT

The scriptwriter outlined some visual elements in the script. Let's say you're producing a new product introduction. A narrator talks to the audience about how great the product is, broken up at intervals by a description of the product and a list of all its features and benefits. The program is not very technical or sophisticated, but only because the writer is counting on you and the production company to add material that will supplement what he's already included. Where do you go from here?

Consider using the following:

1. On-camera narrator
2. Print material
3. Computer graphics
4. Location inserts
5. Keycards
6. Company props
7. Archive footage
8. Pre-packaged special effects
9. Slides
10. Photographs
11. Backdrops
12. Foam board
13. Promotional videos
14. Costumes
15. Miscellaneous props and devices
16. U-think-they-build

1. *On-camera narrator*
Wait a minute. Didn't you and the scriptwriter already decide to use on-camera talent?

Well, yes and no. You may have decided to use on-camera talent, but the script won't always tell you when the talent appears, and when only a voice is heard. That's because the writer designed the narrative to be flexible. It tells your producer that yes, at this point the talent can be seen showing the audience how to use an encyclopedia, but if the producer feels that a step-by-step list would work better, then only the talent's voice is needed.

The key is to have the talent appear often enough to give the program credibility, without becoming a talking head. Read through the audio portion of the script and select descriptive paragraphs. These may include:

- Lists of features and benefits
- Points and highlights
- Names and addresses

- Procedures
- Explanations

In other words, you want to emphasize key ideas that, when reinforced with graphics, will teach or motivate. The next question is, when should the talent share the screen with this information, when should a list or procedure appear on its own, and when should the talent just talk about it?

> *Example 1.* The narrator of a computer training program reminds viewers that in order to get the best possible service from the company's technical support division, they should have their software program and version, registration number, and information about their computer at the ready so the support rep can help them solve a problem quickly and efficiently. In this case it would be better to show a list of these requirements on its own than have the narrator tell them about it.

> *Example 2.* The narrator of a public service video emphasizes that only one government agency can give the viewers the help they need. Because this a strong message, having the name and address of the agency appear at the bottom of the screen while the narrator is speaking provides authority. The narrator is urging viewers to take action.

> *Example 3.* The narrator of an auto repair video tells viewers to check the oil in their cars on a regular basis. Rather than having a list explain how to do this, the narrator lifts up the hood, shows viewers where the dipstick is, and then demonstrates how use it.

Try out these variations with your house producer. You may give her a fresh perspective on how to shoot a scene.

2. *Print material*

By print material I mean anything having to do with your program. This includes brochures and sales kits, contracts, textbooks, and manuals. Have these items ready for your shoot. If your marketing, sales, or training department has to get them from another source, put in your order early.

You're going to need at least three of everything. During production and post-production, print material will be cut, taped, tacked, or stapled to a surface for the camera to get in close, or to provide a shot of all the material together. It may also be handled by the narrator or actors. Wrinkles, creases, bends, and tears should be anticipated. Be prepared!

3. *Computer graphics*

Now let's add computer graphics.

Also known as "CGs," computer graphics can be as simple as words, lines, and phrases popping up on the screen as the narrator speaks, or as complex as having the words come to life from the very pages of the print material.

If you watch television commercials carefully, you'll see words grow, mutate, and dissipate from every corner of the screen, along with every prop and actor, out of thin air. These sophisticated effects are done in the editing suite, and that's where you'll spend an inordinate amount of money if you're not careful. The really impressive special effects come from very advanced machinery, technology that for all the ooohing and aaahing does not come cheap.

For the purposes of your program, a simple character generator will do the job. This is nothing more than a keyboard, a small monitor so you can see what you're doing, and some fonts and colors. Most are quite easy to learn and use. If you get the chance, give it a try.

4. *Location inserts*

Think about adding location inserts. These don't have to be fancy or expensive. How about shooting the company building? Maybe you'd like a street scene. How about people in your company at work?

Even if you haven't left any time in your schedule to shoot them, the production company can easily take a few hours out of its day to do it. They're easy because they don't necessarily require an audio track. The less equipment required, the easier the shoot is.

Why would you want to add location inserts? You want to show that your company is innovative. You want to show hard-working people, especially if you're shooting in a home office. A street scene shows the diversity of your clientele. Spread out over appropriate points in the script, location inserts add realism and immediacy to the program.

5. *Keycards*

Want to add a distinctive touch to your program? Have a keycard made of your company name and logo.

A keycard is very easy to make. Your company already has letterhead, and in some cases a logo. This logo should be camera-ready; that is, a sharp black image of the logo set against a white background. The production company or a graphic arts studio will take that artwork and reproduce it for a video camera's visual dimensions on a piece of foam board. When completed, the logo and title will be white and placed against a black background.

A keycard can be quite handy. When placed on-camera, the logo can be superimposed in reverse video (keyed) over a scene that has already been taped or is being taped with another camera.

For example: Let's say you want to start the program with an exterior shot of the company building. You also want to identify it. A CG would work, but chances are the character generator would not be able to match your company title's font or recreate the logo.

Using a keycard, the editor will superimpose your company's title and logo over the building shot. When done in this way, the keycard image will show up as black type against the screen image (the type can be manipulated to take on other colors as well). If you use a camera motion such as a zoom in and combine it with a fade-in, the result will be one of motion. Your logo will appear to have come out of nowhere.

Another use for the keycard involves two cameras. One camera is set on a primary visual, such as the narrator. The keycard is shot with the second camera. Now you can mix the company's title and logo with the narrator whenever you want.

Using a keycard is optional, of course. Many companies produce fine programs using well-chosen fonts for their company title, and leave out the logo altogether. The choice is yours.

6. *Company props*

Think of the studio set you'll be shooting in. Will the narrator be standing in front of a backdrop? Will you need an office set? A stool for the narrator to sit on?

The set should always be secondary to the action. But even props can be useful. If the narrator is picking up a brochure or any other sales material from a desk, you'll want the desk to look authentic. Huge nicks and cigarette burns on a washed-out tabletop or side panel will definitely distract from the words.

Consider other props: a blackboard or bulletin board, chart stand, hand-held reports/testimonials, or incentive gifts. Maybe there's a commemorative gift from the last sales conference that can be used.

Sales people expect their home office to look a certain way. They expect operating departments to look busy and, yes, even cluttered. Clean desks arouse suspicion. Family photographs should adorn credenzas. Evidence of activity should abound. After all, sales reps work hard for their money, and they expect the same from you.

Little visual touches make a difference. If your talent is acting out the part of a sales rep, think about a sales office. What would a rep have on her desk? Would she use a company pen? Would the latest sales contest poster hang in the background? What about inspirational trinkets, those clever sayings and statuettes and buttons?

7. *Archive footage*

You've now assembled a formidable array of visual elements that you can arrange in any order and style you want, but let's go a couple of steps further.

If you're thinking about using historical images, or location footage that would be difficult to obtain through a production service, consider using a film archive.

These companies have thousands of film images that can be transferred to video. They can be of varying lengths, subjects, and eras. Used to make a special point or comparison, they can add nostalgia or emotion to the script.

An archive usually has a catalog of images for you to choose from, along with their original running times. The staff can either run off a rough copy of the selected images or have you come in to look at them. When the final choices are made, they use a high-quality film-to-tape transfer machine to give you a master to work from in the editing suite.

8. *Pre-packaged special effects*

Another option is to use pre-packaged special effects. Some companies produce whole series of tapes filled with hundreds of bits of animation, computer-designed backgrounds, and camera effects. Check to see if the production company or editing suite has any of these tapes available.

Your choices may range from one- and two-second flashes of light to sunsets lasting several minutes. Each tape contains at least three or four different-length versions of the same effect. Each effect also ends with just enough pause or static frame to allow for repeats. If the flashy computer bulletin board you like only lasts a minute, but your text lasts for three, you can tag the effect onto itself to extend its playing time.

Placing text over a moving background or static yet colorful background makes any information you present livelier, and in some cases creates indelible images that will bring your message home. If you're going on a cruise and you put contest rules over a picture of a moving boat, your audience will remember the message.

9. *Slides*

A collective groan rises from the peanut gallery; not another boring slide show! Have mercy on us!

It's not quite what you think. Using a slide as a static background while you roll information across the screen will work, and quite effectively. Perhaps a photographer took a few dozen shots of a manager's recent presentation. Maybe a studio made some slides with the company name and logo. Perhaps a graded background or other special effect is sitting in someone's slide tray right now. By all means use it! The production company can have slides transferred to video. You never know when a slide will find a new and useful life.

10. *Photographs*

Like slides, stock photos can add a nice background to any text. A sharp image transfers well when placed on-camera. Some photo supply stores carry a library of pictures and can take you around the world.

When is a good time to use photographs? Sales contests work well, particularly if the company is giving away a car or a tropical vacation. High-tech equipment and computers also qualify. If only one office in the country is using a Cray-1 computer, there's no sense sending a crew 2,000 miles to shoot ten seconds' worth of tape.

Use your judgement. There's certainly nothing wrong with using a static shot. But as with any presentation, too much of one thing leads to rapid boredom. How many times have you sat through an endless slide show or page after page of overheads?

With this in mind, you'll have no problem breaking up your script into entertaining and informative segments.

11. *Backdrops*

For most people, a backdrop is a heavy piece of black or blue material that hangs behind the narrator, a bland, light-absorbing effect that makes your video look like a driver's license.

Welcome to the modern world. Today's backdrop is whatever you want it to be. Need a three-dimensional forest? No problem. Could you use the city's skyline for your news show? Just ask. Got something on your mind, an image captured from a surrealistic dream? Well, that might take an extra day.

You'll find one of the most famous backdrops of them all at Universal Studios in California. Just down the road from the Psycho House, a very large pool of water sits before an enormous backdrop of the sky, wisps of clouds and all. Universal uses this set when it films ocean scenes. It's so convincing that from the right distance you can't tell where the backdrop ends and the sky begins. That's how good today's backdrops are.

12. *Foam board*

We've already discussed the use of foam board when we had a keycard made, but its uses are many. Home exteriors, fences, machinery and other common, everyday items can be fashioned out of foam board. And there's very little loss in realism if done properly. The best part is that they are easy to move around and store. And they don't cost anywhere near the real thing.

13. *Promotional videos*

Hotels, conference centers, travel agencies, and just about anyone else with a vested interest in attracting business has a promotional video waiting to be viewed.

Years ago I wrote and produced a contest video offering sales reps a free trip to Florida. For most of the sales force—residents of the north—this was an exotic trip, and the hotel accommodations were said to be nothing short of an emperor's palace. All they had to do to get there was meet a quarterly sales quota.

To give the contest a look that would inspire greater sales, I obtained a thirty-minute promotional video from the hotel, a well-known facility noted for its architectural splendors and abundance of activities. By inserting choice sections of the tape into the script, the promotion took viewers on a trip far from their wintry offices to the warmth and excitement of the Florida coast. It was a program that people talked about.

Promotional videos are great to use because they contain more than enough material to spread out over a series of programs. As long as you inform your sources that you'll be reproducing the material for internal use only, you won't encounter any resistance to its unlimited use. To them, it's free advertising. The more people who see it, the better.

14. *Costumes*

Your industry probably covers a large and varied segment of society. Your clients are working people, and working people take on various roles.

As your scripts become more sophisticated, you may reach a point where one of your actors or actresses plays the part of an employee or client on the job. Whether the role is a surgeon or a telephone line repair person, the talent must look the part. Throwing on a pair of jeans, painter's gloves, or tennis shoes won't convince too many people that the character climbs wooden poles or performs surgery for a living.

Make sure your actor dresses the part.

- If the talent will portray a surgeon, and you work for a hospital, contact your supply department.
- If your script takes you into another business, like a foundry, have the house producer contact the company's owner or manager to borrow the proper attire.
- If you really need something unusual, like a 1960s-style space suit, consult your creative directory for a listing of costume services or ask your producer to find one for you.

15. *Miscellaneous props and devices*

This is a business that loves a challenge, and chances are someone will have what you want.

The following list merely scratches the surface of what's available. Some services are expensive, and others require trained professionals to operate. But they're there for you any time you need them.

- Prosthetics
- Banners
- Murals
- Crystal
- Silver
- Ice Cubes
- Pyrotechnics
- Weapons
- Homes
- Streets
- Food
- Animals
- Cabinets
- Streetlamps
- Chandeliers
- Rugs
- Paintings
- Sculptures
- Tapestries

- Fog/rain
- Snow/grass
- Rocks
- Lasers
- Machines
- Autos
- Dancefloors
- Jewelry
- Musical instruments

16. *U-think-they-build*

Go ahead. Give someone a sketch of a marvelous invention that will add the right touch to your program on changing technologies, and let the wizards do their thing. As long as you stay within the boundaries of physics and good taste, someone can make your ideas come alive.

These are just a few examples of the types of visual elements you can use. Obviously, you don't want to use them all in every program, and you certainly don't want to use them too much in one program. Dazzling the audience is one thing, but if the people walk away not knowing what they've just seen, all the special effects in the world won't be worth the loss of a message.

Once again, let's look at our visual choices:

1. On-camera narrator
2. Print material
3. Computer graphics
4. Location inserts
5. Keycards
6. Company props
7. Archive footage
8. Pre-packaged special effects
9. Slides
10. Photographs
11. Backdrops
12. Foam board
13. Promotional videos
14. Costumes
15. Miscellaneous props and devices
16. U-think-they-build

Are we done yet? Not really. As you work your way through a few productions you'll see how camera angles, filters, and lighting can add their own look to a scene.

Working with the scriptwriter and your producer can produce some truly satisfying programs if everyone agrees to leave the creative door open.

Right now it seems like a lot to coordinate, but it doesn't need to be a chore. The people you're working with will be happy to discuss new and different ways of presenting your material. Have some fun with it!

AT THIS STAGE OF THE PRE-PRODUCTION PROCESS YOU SHOULD

- Review your production. (Have you met with the production company to discuss the script and talent? Have you set and confirmed dates for taping and editing?)
- Make a list of visual elements you can add to your production, or have the production company locate them for you.
- Be flexible and open to new ways of seeing things.

STEP 3

Production

10

Managing Your Production in the Studio

With all of the pieces in place, the big studio day finally arrives.

Until now, just about everything you've dealt with has been on paper—the treatment, production calendar, script, talent photos and resumés, and pre-production notes. But in the studio, these ingredients are combined in measured portions to create something greater than the sum of its parts.

Your first responsibility is to ensure the integrity of the script and the manner in which it is brought to the screen. You also represent your company. The people you work with in the studio may be more knowledgeable about the video business than you are, but in the end you sign the checks, and they know that.

There is a basic etiquette you should always follow when working in a studio. When all sides play by the rules, a shoot is enjoyable and a wonderful learning experience for all. When common courtesies are ignored, prepare yourself for a very long day.

STUDIO ETIQUETTE FOR PRODUCERS

1. Studio technicians know the quickest and most efficient ways to prepare a studio for taping. Too often clients will read a couple of video magazines or attend a few seminars and think they now have the expertise to tell technicians where to put the camera and how the lights should be set up. Stay out of the way and let them do what they do best.

2. The director is in charge of the production (for the remainder of this book, I am assuming that your house producer is also your program's director). Working from the script, the director will have mapped out camera angles with the diversity necessary to keep the visual portion of the show fresh. Unless there is a gross visual error, such as seating a sales rep between prospects or showing a closeup of an incorrect form, your input should be limited.
3. The talent are skilled and professional. While you have some say over pronunciations, gestures, and looks, they know what works and what doesn't. They already know how to sell. Let them help you shape the program.

STUDIO ETIQUETTE FOR THE PRODUCTION STAFF

Yes, you have rights, too. It is rare to find studio personnel who are unwilling to listen to what you have to say, even if this is the first time you've ever set foot on a soundstage.

1. As a producer, you represent your company. An actor can play a scene brilliantly, then suddenly ad-lib the last line. Sometimes this works to your show's advantage, and sometimes it doesn't. If you feel the message of a particular scene has been overshadowed by an on-camera change in the script, you have the right to ask that it be shot again.
2. The director should ask for your OK on every scene. You should have discussed the overall look of the production during pre-production, but the director should still consult with you on the on-camera look. If a scene doesn't look right, have the camera moved or the talent shifted until it does.
3. Studio technicians must give you the look you want. As we previously discussed, a sales rep's desk must look authentic for the scene to establish any credibility. Never accept a set that doesn't ring true. Even if it upsets the technicians' lighting scheme, that's a matter for them to deal with.

A well-executed production will already have this etiquette built in. There may be occasions where you'll run into uncooperative personnel, but always hold your ground. As long as your company is paying for these services, you have the power to grant or deny requests.

There are, of course, well-documented tales of horror a production company or talent will tell you about the Client from Hell. Many productions have been shot over and over again over a period of months because of vacillating desires on the part of the client. In a way the production company doesn't really care because it just rings up another few thousand dollars on the final bill, but it also eats up valuable opportunities to work with other clients.

Moderation and balance require give and take on all sides. Mutual respect is critical; working together produces programs of inspiration and creativity. See the production for what it is—a means of communicating valuable information to an appreciative audience.

The next section walks through some of the elements of production day. With a few exceptions, you will be called upon to make decisions on every issue.

TALENT WARDROBE

Customarily, the talent will bring to the taping at least three suits, along with shirts, blouses, ties, and shoes. The talent knows that your video requires a professional look, and will undoubtedly ask you which outfit best suits your company's personality.

That call is up to you, but there are guidelines you should observe. Unlike our own visual capabilities, the video camera does not blink or lie, and can in fact be downright cruel. When combined with lights and a set, what looks like an innocuous outfit out in the hallway can suddenly look bland and ugly when the tape begins to roll. A little prevention now saves a lot of trouble later.

On-Camera Dress Tips

1. Avoid color extremes. Stay away from black, white, orange, and red. Bright colors will flare or strobe on-camera; that is, any motion by the talent will result in a smear across the screen. This is called a flare. Strobing colors vibrate and are very hard on the eyes. Pastels and colors in the mid-range of the spectrum work best. These include gray, blue, brown, maroon, purple, and forest green.
2. Avoid patterns such as checks, stripes, herringbone, or plaid. I can assure you that a pattern will drive the camera crazy and the image will vibrate so much it will give any viewer an instant headache.
3. Put the jewelry away. Likewise, do not allow sequins or any metallic-looking material such as lamé. These reflect light very easily.
4. Keep the outfit simple. A jacket with an embroidered patch on one side is distracting. Also stay away from shirts with logos and pictures unless the scene specifically calls for it.

Clothes should make the talent look professional and part of your management team. Outfits should be comfortable and very much in line with the company's dress code. A tight-fitting muscle shirt or a low-necklined dress is not acceptable attire. Ties should have simple, solid colors. For women, bows are fine but scarves should be avoided.

I once saw a training program that used two narrators, one of whom was a woman who wore a very large scarf draped around her neck. Every time a new scene began and the camera focused in on her, the scarf was in a different position. The result was unintentionally hilarious—the scarf, throughout the course of the show, made several revolutions around the woman's neck. Once the audience had discovered this, that's what the people watched for, laughing out loud whenever she appeared on the screen. The program's message was lost. The scarf was the only thing they remembered.

The rules for on-camera attire appear rigid and not very creative, but they do provide a place to start. Just because the list warns you away from stripes does not mean you have to exclude all stripes. A very fine pinstripe on a gray or blue suit will work just fine.

Your talent knows what to avoid and will not present any outfits that might cause visual distractions. Using company talent will require you to make these guidelines known ahead of time.

MAKEUP

Again, the talent is experienced enough to apply makeup without help. This includes face powder, lipstick, and eye shadow.

Face powder is the most essential makeup because studio lights will make talent perspire. Shiny areas on the face—hot spots—will reflect light as much as any jewelry. These areas fall mostly on the nose and forehead. During the course of the shoot, the talent may take a moment to reapply any makeup should the director pick up any potential hot spots on the monitor.

Lipstick is a simple matter—less is better. A basic color to help highlight the face is okay, but it should match the outfit. Loud colors, no matter how fashionable, are not acceptable. Eye makeup should follow suit. You'd be surprised how quickly talent can look like a raccoon when a little too much mascara is applied.

Hairstyle is as important as the outfit. You'll find that most talent wear their hair in a simple, unadorned manner. A big commercial shoot may require a special style (for which there are professional stylists on hand), but for your purposes a simple cut will do. Longer hair should be pinned back or to one side. Like a scarf, long hair can do amazing things if left unchecked.

There are some minor considerations to remember, though they are no less important. Male talent should be clean-shaven; a five o'clock shadow is unsightly. For women, nail polish should be clear. For both, manicured hands—especially if closeups are involved—are essential.

CAN YOU READ THIS?

We now turn our attention to the means by which the script will be delivered to the audience. Will the talent use a teleprompter, an ear prompter, or memorize the lines?

The teleprompter is the most common way of reading a script. Your local newscaster uses one. The teleprompter is a screen placed in front of the camera that scrolls text to match the user's reading speed. The screen does not interfere with the camera's ability to record the talent, and the text can be "rolled back" if another take is needed. All talent know how to use a teleprompter.

One drawback to using a teleprompter is that of motion. Simply put, the talent can't move around very much because the teleprompter gets harder to read. Some teleprompters are also very big and awkward. A camera may have a difficult time giving you a smooth pan or tilt because the teleprompter is putting a lot of weight on the tripod or camera stand.

Another problem has to do with the text. A paper-fed teleprompter is difficult to edit because it requires writing on the paper. Ink is harder to read than type. Electronic text creation and editing is easier.

An ear prompter requires more skill. First, the talent pre-records the script into a microcassette recorder. After the recorder is attached to a belt or placed in a pocket, one line is run behind the neck as the earpiece, and another is run down the arm and into the palm for manual control.

When the tape rolls, the cassette is activated. The talent listens to the script and repeats the words a fraction of a second later. The result is quite impressive—the talent is able to hear and comprehend the script and repeat it at the same time, word for word, with incredible accuracy. Not all talent can do this, and many choose not to.

An ear prompter has its limitations, too. Since the talent has already recorded the script before the shoot, any changes performed on the set will have to be re-recorded. This takes time, especially if whole new sections of text are added. And while most ear pieces are virtually unnoticeable, a turn of the head or a glint of light may reveal how the talent is able to remember so much text.

The third method is for the talent to memorize the script. If you're shooting short segments in which a sales rep asks questions and the prospects answer, memorization works well. Long scripts with lengthy scenes do not easily lend themselves to memorization.

Each of these methods has its place and usefulness. You may want to bring this up during your pre-production meeting. Some actors prefer to use ear prompters; others like working with teleprompters. The bottom line here is that personal comfort goes a long way in keeping studio shoots short and sweet. Never try to force actors to use one method if they tell you up front that they prefer to use another.

MICROPHONES

Watching old B-movies on late-night television provides more than its fair share of amusement, but even the worst of them will have a decent soundtrack. It may contain the wrong sounds, but at least they can be heard.

Studio microphones come in four basic types:

1.   *The wireless.* This microphone is about the size of a dime and is attached to the underside of a tie or lapel. It is connected to a small transmitter, which relays the signal to a receiver hooked into the studio's audio system.

A wireless is best used when the talent needs to walk around without tripping over wires. On the down side, friction between certain fabrics can produce scraping and brushing sounds that will come through loud and clear.

2.   *The boom.* This is a microphone attached to a long pole suspended above the head of the talent. The pole may be hand-held or attached to a stand. Talk shows and motion pictures often use this type of microphone.

Keep in mind, however, that the camera frame will show the microphone if it is brought too close to the talent. And as the microphone is pulled away, there is a resultant loss of voice quality. Make sure the person using the boom is experienced.

3.   *The shotgun.* This is a hand-held microphone consisting of a hand grip and a long barrel, used in place of a boom. A sound technician may be placed near the talent but is kept out of the frame. Documentaries and standup outdoor interviews make good use of this microphone.

4.   *The handheld.* Talk show hosts will carry this type of microphone around with them as they work an audience, and news reporters rely on them for field reports, but few studio productions will require talent to use one. They can be unwieldy and are not very practical, especially if the talent has to pick up or hold something with the other hand.

No matter which you use, all microphones come with a windscreen. This cuts down on extraneous noises such as the wind, the popping and hissing of the letters P and S, or the hum of a central air conditioning unit, but they do not filter out unwanted sounds like an air hammer pounding into a wall thirty feet away.

Voiceover microphones come in different shapes and sizes, but their look is not as important because there's no camera to deal with. What is important is the way they capture and transmit the human voice.

Before any scenes are shot, the director and studio engineer will perform a series of thorough sound checks. Once shooting begins, you may notice that the volume in the control room (where you'll watch the action) is set higher than you think is necessary, but it makes unwanted sounds easier to catch. No one is trying to make you deaf or scare you away.

LIGHTING

In real life we cast shadows, whether we are outdoors or in an office. On video, shadows have no place unless called for by the script.

Think of a television commercial shot inside a home or business. You'll notice that shadows simply do not exist, even on a sunny day at the beach. Strange but true. Even stranger, however, are those movies where the actors cast double shadows, one from the sun, and the other from the lights. Someone was obviously not doing his job.

There are whole volumes dedicated to the use of lighting. The right combination of lights can make a scene look friendly or sinister. Talent can look energetic or tired. Products can stand out from the crowd or elicit jaded yawns.

For every need, there is a light. There are quartz, tungsten, and carbon lamps, among others. There are lights that intensify and lights that soften. There are "barn door" attachments that shape the beam of light, and there are gobos, scrims, flags, and cookies.

The most basic style of studio lighting is called three-point lighting. As you might imagine, lights are set up at three different points, each light illuminating a portion of the subject and canceling out the shadows created by the other two. When all three lights are used together, all shadows are eliminated from the set and the subject appears to be speaking to us from what we perceive to be a normal, three-dimensional setting.

As your productions become more complex—involving motion and numerous subjects—your lighting scheme will follow suit. This includes shooting outdoors, as well as the use of natural lighting, which offers a whole new set of rules.

SETS AND PROPS

We've already discussed the need to make a sales rep's desk look like one, and the same goes for an executive's office, a prospect's living room, and any other scene called for in the script. For the most part, a studio will provide basic set pieces, but you will be expected to make a contribution.

Look around for things you can beg or borrow from the office—small bookends and a few sales-related volumes, phone books and memo pads, file folders and calculators, and picture frames and trinkets. Pack these items carefully and make a note of your inventory. It's easy to forget what belongs to whom and your benefactors will no doubt want their items back when you're done.

As with the talent's wardrobe, you should be aware that props and certain parts of the set can be distracting. Metal objects reflect the most light, but often a glass or crystal ornament can also cause problems.

If it's necessary to have some reflective object in the scene, a technician will apply a spray to it that cuts the sharpness of its reflection. Sometimes a piece of tape on the arm of a metal chair will also cut glare.

In a previous chapter we discussed using print material as a prop the narrator can hold up or refer to. Again, be sure to bring a lot of copies in case something gets wrinkled or torn. Better to have too much than too little.

CONTINUITY

This sounds simple enough, but over the course of a production it can be easy to lose track of your scenes.

An example: You're watching a movie, and in one particular scene our hero and heroine are seated at a dining room table with an open bottle of wine between them. The scene cuts away to a closeup of the hero's face as he talks, then cuts away to the heroine as she talks. When the camera cuts back to the two of them seated at the table, the bottle of wine is now corked.

What happened? When movies are shot, scenes are filmed out of sequence. That is, if the start of the movie takes place in a kitchen and the movie ends in the kitchen, those scenes are shot on the same day or series of days. Within a scene, the director will shoot what's called an establishing shot, in this case our couple sitting at a table having a conversation and corking an open bottle of wine. The next scene is shot with a closeup of the man repeating his dialogue from the establishing shot, and the same is done with the woman. When edited together, it appears that the conversation is flowing effortlessly between the establishing shot and the two actors. The problem of continuity in this case is that in repeating their dialogue for the cutaway shots, one of the actors didn't reach over and cork the bottle of wine to match the establishing shot.

Since movies are not filmed as a linear sequence of events, continuity between scenes becomes important. In fact, as you watch the credits of any movie, you'll find someone who is in charge of continuity. As scenes are shot, she stands around with a clipboard making notes such as in which hand someone is holding a cigarette, which way the character is looking or moving, and other considerations.

Failure to pay close attention to the action will create problems in the editing suite. One way to reduce the chance of something slipping by is to limit the number of items in a scene that will be moved.

Shooting out of sequence is an efficient way of putting a show together. Let's say you're doing a news program. You have two anchors but only one camera to work with. Within the program you will have three separate shots: a close shot of Anchor #1, a close shot of Anchor #2, and a two-shot with both anchors.

If you were in a TV studio, this would be easy because there's more

than one camera, each focused on a different anchor. You don't have that luxury, and you need to maximize your studio time so you don't have to reset the camera every time an anchor speaks his lines.

The solution is simple. First you set and shoot all the scenes that require both anchors. You then reset the camera to shoot all of the scenes requiring only Anchor #1 (the other anchor can leave the studio floor), then reset the camera again for all scenes requiring only Anchor #2.

When the program is put together in editing—for example, a two-shot of both anchors followed by a close shot of Anchor #1 reading his story to a close shot of Anchor #2 doing the same—it will appear as if there are three cameras in the studio, and that all of the scenes are spontaneous, just like a live news broadcast.

TAKE THAT!

While you're keeping a firm and consistent grip on continuity from scene to scene, you'll also have to deal with the challenge of multiple takes.

Many things can go wrong during a scene. The talent can trip over the words, a boom mike can suddenly appear in the frame, the audio will mysteriously fade out, and a multitude of other things. Accept this as part of the production process. Doing a scene five or six times is not designed to drive you insane but to capture the essence of the program.

As a scene is shot, your attention span will be stretched to the limit. You have to follow along with the script, make sure the talent is gesturing and using props properly, and that every scene looks as good as the scene before. This is not an easy task, especially for a beginner.

After a scene is shot, you will sometimes have the opportunity to see it again. The director will frequently have the tape rolled back to watch how it turned out, and often base a retake on a gut feeling or to correct a mistake. If you're not sure what you saw or heard, ask for a playback.

TIME OUT

The length and complexity of the script determine how much time is needed in the studio. For a six-minute new product introduction, for example, you will need only a day or less to shoot the necessary scenes. If that seems long for only a few pages of text, keep in mind that a studio setup takes time. When that's added to multiple takes, camera resets, and audio checks, it's best not to be in a hurry.

The only time you're going to need two or more days of shooting is if you require the talent to read part of the script from a location other than the studio or if the script is very long, as in a series of training tapes.

It is important for your superiors back at the office to understand the amount of time that you will need to spend in the studio. As I said earlier, video is a time-consuming medium. Support for your position as producer can wane quickly if someone thinks you're spending too much time away from the office. So before you immerse yourself in the studio, make sure you give someone the studio phone number and a rough idea how long you'll be there. If the shoot runs into technical problems and it looks like you'll be longer than you thought, call in.

While you're at it, it will be absolutely essential for someone at your company to be available to answer any questions that may come up during the taping. Despite the many levels of authority a script must pass through on its way to completion, inadvertent mistakes do crop up from time to time. For example, let's say that you mention a 6 percent sales commission on page one of the script, but later on you say that the commission is a variable based on specific volumes of product sold. Which is correct?

Clarification here will help. It could very well be that the 6 percent commission is an average based on a projected volume of individual sales. In this situation, both versions are correct, but only one should be clearly stated in the script. Which version is more important?

ALL TOGETHER NOW

Let's review our day in the studio:

1. The director and studio technicians have assembled a simple set consisting of a desk in a typical office environment. Print material is within easy reach of the talent.
2. The talent arrives and you do your part by suggesting that she wear a blue suit. She will be reading off a teleprompter, and just to make sure there are no surprises along the way, you point out some minor changes that have been made to the script.
3. The talent gets into costume. She stands before the camera as the lights are adjusted, the teleprompter is tested, and a sound check is performed. The director goes over last-minute instructions with the talent and crew.
4. With everything ready to go, the tape rolls, and the talent reads the script. Several retakes are necessary. After each scene, the director has the tape rolled back to briefly check its look and to make sure the delivery was crisp and clear.
5. Once the audio portion of the program is completed, the director shoots some insert shots of the talent's hands holding a presentation packet. You make sure the talent holds it in the same hand as in a previous scene.
6. When you and the director are satisfied with the program's look, the

talent is dismissed and the tapes are marked according to scenes and set aside for editing.

This is the simplest way of describing a shoot, and depending on who you're working with, there may be short breaks taken between scenes, deli platters for an attack of the munchies, and time taken out for phone calls and dealing with other business matters. It all hinges on how much production time was scheduled. I've had intense two-hour shoots that went straight into editing and six-hour shoots that were more like a leisurely picnic than a serious endeavor. You won't know until it happens. Once baptized by the experience of working in a studio, you'll get a better feel for the next production. You'll understand the visual aspects of a script much better and you'll develop little touches that add personality to potentially dry material.

With our studio shoot complete, the next day or two will be spent on location, one of the most challenging aspects of any production.

AT THIS STAGE OF THE PRODUCTION PROCESS YOU SHOULD

- Prepare for your day in the studio. Assemble all print material and company props, and let someone know where you can be reached.
- Follow the rules of studio etiquette before, during, and after taping.
- Make sure your talent is dressed according to your company's image.
- Note how the production company makes use of teleprompters and ear prompters, microphones, lighting, and the set.
- Practice the art of continuity to ensure that scenes will match up later in the editing suite.
- Make sure someone in your company will be available to answer questions.

11

Managing Your Production on Location

Location shooting is without a doubt the most exciting and rewarding experience a producer can have. It's also the strangest and most chaotic part of any production.

Location work has its own unique characteristics. You're not bound by an artificial set, which gives you and the director greater flexibility, freedom, and creativity. You can add realism and immediacy to the script. You can get people in your company involved as extras. And when a sunrise breaks over early morning clouds just as the talent talks about a new dawn, the spontaneity of capturing the moment is exhilarating.

That's the exciting and rewarding part. Once you leave the safety and predictability of the studio, however, your ability to control events diminishes greatly. You're at the mercy of the weather. Just as you're wrapping up that big office scene, someone steps around the corner and yells, "Hey, Dave, where the @#!* is that report I asked you for?" People trip over cables. And when the crew members finally set up that living room shot and power up all their equipment, every fuse in the house explodes from the surge.

Bring along plenty of patience, be amenable to change, and expect the unexpected. With proper planning, your location shoots will give you the look and feel you want while minimizing potential mishaps.

131

WHAT DO YOU MEAN BY ON LOCATION?

This chapter covers four types of location shooting:

1. Shooting in your company
2. Shooting in another company
3. Shooting in a home
4. Shooting outdoors

Each of these will be covered as a separate topic. We'll walk through a basic setup, discuss what to expect from the production company, and what the production company will expect from you. I'll also provide tips on maintaining continuity from scene to scene, and how you can assist the director and crew.

WHO'S RESPONSIBLE FOR WHAT?

No matter where you're shooting, both you and the production company share in the responsibility for making location work successful.

What You Need to Provide

- Script and production book
- Any props or visuals the talent will need (brochures, manuals, etc.)
- Permission to shoot a department within your company
- Permission to use employees as extras
- Transportation for yourself to the location site

What the Production Company Provides

- Equipment and crew
- Scripts for talent and production assistants
- Talent
- Permission to shoot in another company
- Permits from a local government or municipality
- Certificate of insurance
- Directions to the location site

If you don't have a particular location in mind for a scene such as a hospital, law firm, or home, the production company staff will either scout out a suitable location for you or use a location already familiar to them. In any event, get detailed directions and leave enough time to get to the site. Location shooting often begins early in the day when rush hour traffic is at its worst. Don't be late.

SHOOTING IN YOUR COMPANY

Let's get one thing out of the way before we proceed. Yes, this is your big chance to show off in front of your co-workers and boss and impress the vice-president. Don't tell me the thought hasn't occurred to you. Now that we've cleared the air, let's get down to business.

Shooting a department and its employees demands a lot of input from you. The director and crew will count on you to show them where a scene will take place, what activities are performed, and most of all, where all the outlets are. Portable recorders come equipped with battery packs, but whenever possible crews prefer to plug in. They'll bring extension cords with them, so don't feel you have to set up the camera and lights next to the nearest wall socket.

During pre-production you and the house producer read through the script and decided that one or more scenes required the following:

A. Scenes with on-camera talent
B. Scenes without the talent and without an audio track
C. Scenes without the talent but with background audio

A. Scenes with On-Camera Talent

This is the trickiest to pull off. This usually requires the talent to stand or walk around while explaining to the audience what's going on behind her. While the director maps out the talent's movements and runs through the scene a few times, you can get involved by making sure that the scene itself is completed quickly without disrupting normal work flow. For example: If the talent needs to walk past a couple of desks and stop in front of someone's work station, have the phone volume turned down or the calls transferred. You want to show activity, of course, but you don't want to keep reshooting the scene because a chorus of piercing rings drowns out the narrative.

Get the employees involved in the scene by having them watch the run-throughs and explain what's going to happen. Why? It's a natural inclination to "sneak a peek" at a camera and talent when taping commences. The scene should look natural, as if the talent does not exist and the workers are merely going about their day-to-day business.

Don't get in anyone's way. You may shoot in areas that have a limited amount of space. The room may have only one exit. If more than two or three people need to move around near your setup, have power cords taped to the floor.

Get the department manager to make an appearance. Background action is good, but adding managerial involvement is better. Having a manager walk into a scene to discuss business with an associate shows that your company cares about its people.

Once the scene is ready for a take, position yourself to one side of the camera where you can get a good view of the action, but be out of the crew's way. The crew members will be absorbed in their own functions, as will the camera operator and director, focused mostly on the talent. This is where you can offer additional assistance.

- Look out for unexpected shadows. The lights were set and checked based on current activity. Someone suddenly getting up from a desk may cast enough of a shadow to make the lighting scheme obvious. Have the tape rolled back and reviewed.
- Watch for glints or flashes of light. Small objects made of metal, glass, and plastic can easily catch a light and create a distracting, momentary glare behind the talent. Start the scene again with the object in question moved.
- Keep an eye out for peekers. Someone is bound to look up at the camera or talent no matter how many times you practice a scene.

As if this were not enough, you also have to make sure the talent reads her lines correctly, with any technical words and phrases properly pronounced, and that her actions look smooth and natural. If it looks like she's having difficulty picking up an object from a desk or points to something in the wrong direction, don't let it pass. Run-throughs are done to make sure every aspect of a scene is flawless. Don't be in a rush and accept even minor errors as okay. It's your show and your company.

One thing you should be absolutely sure of is to have the talent wear the same outfit she wore in the studio. You want to create the illusion of transporting the talent from place to place. Different attire creates a visually jarring effect that separates time and space. The only exception is if the talent has to be dressed in an outfit relevant to a location, like a nuclear power plant.

B. Scenes without the Talent and without an Audio Track

Not all location scenes require the talent to make an appearance. During the studio shoot, the talent may read a few descriptive paragraphs of office activities that are shot at a later time. All the production company has to do is show up at your door and fill in the gaps.

Generally speaking, this an easy shoot. The crew members set up a scene as they would for the talent, only now there is no audio track to record. Each scene is taped for thirty seconds or a minute to give the editor enough tape to work with, there's virtually no rehearsal to perform other than having employees look busy, and you can shoot multiple scenes in less than half the time than if you needed the talent to move around and speak.

As a producer you still have a lot to do, especially if you're shooting more than one scene in more than one area. Before the shoot you must tell managers when to expect the crew to arrive. You don't want to barge in on an important meeting. You should also give them some idea of how long taping will last. Cooperation is one thing, but many managers will lose patience with you if they think you're hanging around too long. Get in, set up, shoot, and get out.

Certain departments should be handled with extreme care. Companies with data processing rooms are not a good place to start pulling plugs and running power lines that could interfere with their operations. If you have to shoot in a power-sensitive area, ask the manager where the best place is to set up. You may have to run extension cords down the hall, but better that than taking a chance of damaging expensive equipment. You don't want to go down in company history as the one who singlehandedly wiped out six months' worth of records.

C. Scenes without the Talent but with Background Audio

The talent again sets up a visual sequence during studio taping, only now you need to have other people talking in order to make a scene work.

For example: The talent talks about the latest trauma treatments available, and you've already cleared permission from your hospital administrator to have a trauma team simulate an emergency. You don't want the talent talking over the scene; you want professionals talking to each other to show how the new technique is applied.

The trauma team knows how to get the job done, and will run through the procedures with the director who will then set the camera in such a way as to capture the moment as realistically as possible. Several takes, closeups, and team shots may be necessary.

Maintaining continuity is critical. So much is going on that it's easy to forget which actors were standing where, what they all had in their hands, and what they were doing, and the director may not catch it all. She may have the people hold their places while the next shot is set up, but in the meantime someone might shift an intravenous bottle from one hand to the other or attach it to a stand.

The scene may be unscripted, as well, which presents its own challenges.

When a shot is completed, make sure the dialogue is completed, too. This is where your knowledge comes in handy. The next shot should pick up where the last instruction was ordered. To help you and the director make the sequence fluid, play back the previous scene for the team so that they can pick up where they left off.

A Final Word about Shooting in Your Company

Do invite your boss and others involved in your project to stop by and watch the action. This will help them understand what goes into a production and give them a chance to meet with the director and talent. A little on-site PR will go a long way to ensure support for this and future productions.

SHOOTING IN ANOTHER COMPANY

Two considerations come to mind: Is this a company associated with your business, staffed by people you know and have worked with on non-video-related projects before, or is this a company the production house contacted to provide background for a scene?

Say your insurance company represents high-risk occupations. That could mean anything from a construction worker to an astronaut. With so many occupations to choose from, the production company may pick one of them for you and make the necessary arrangements to show employees on the job. But if your company recently paid a substantial disability claim to a worker injured on the job, you might want to target that company as the source for your location and get permission to shoot there yourself. Instead of a generic shot of a construction worker, think of the impact you can make by using a company you serve.

The same location options apply in this situation as they did in your own company, shooting with or without the talent, with or without an audio track. You will have to pay particular attention, however, to certain conditions not found in your own company.

- You have to be mindful of the company's willingness to let you shoot at all. In your own company, there is a general understanding that management wants the video shot and expects cooperation from everyone. Complaints are handled through the usual channels. In another company, you're a guest, and any guest can overstay his welcome if the shoot turns out to be more than the hosts bargained for.
- Should the responsibility fall upon you to make location arrangements, talk to the owner or manager about what you want to tape, what the

shoot involves in terms of equipment and personnel, and an estimate of how long it will take. This will not only pave the way for good on-site relations but save you time in the long run. When you describe the scene you want, he may offer suggestions or have an expert on hand to ensure your safety and get the footage you need. He may have his best worker demonstrate a procedure for you or provide the right outfit for the talent to wear. After all, he wants to look good, too. Never turn down any help offered to you.

- Don't insist on changing the way someone does her job to suit an artistic purpose. When a sheet metal worker cuts a piece of steel, there's a reason why it's done a certain way. It may not be pretty or exciting, it's just the most practical way of doing it. It's foolish and downright dangerous to tamper with what works best, and yet I've seen producers and directors take chances "just to get something different."
- Understand that the ebb and flow of another business is unlike your own. You may be confronted with a lot more activity, more people running in and out, phones ringing off the hook, and deliveries being made. Be respectful of the activity around you and do what you can to preserve the energy of the situation.
- In many cases your role may be that of liaison. If a company representative shows up on the set, introduce yourself and answer any questions she might have. If she sees a potential problem, listen to what she has to say and get the director in on the discussion.

SHOOTING IN A HOME

This is about as close to shooting in a studio as you'll find on location and will not seem as hectic or rushed as shooting a busy company department or business. There are things you can do, however, to help move the shoot along:

- Have your visuals ready. Bring along brochures, books, or whatever else the talent will need.
- Stay out of the crew's way. A living room or kitchen looks big enough at first, but once the crew starts setting up, boxes, cables, lights, and other equipment will quickly fill the area. Once you've established where the scene will take place, leave the room.
- While the crew is busy setting up, go over the scene with the director and talent. For example: The scene requires a financial planning expert to show a couple how an investment product can diversify their portfolio. This is where you come in. Explain how everyone is to be seated at a kitchen table or on a living room couch for the presentation; for example, you don't want to seat the rep between the prospects. If the rep uses a

sales presentation book, show the talent how the book is placed on the table and how to use a pen to point out product highlights.

• Answer any questions the talent may have. As you explain how the scene should work, you may be asked how the talent should react to a situation. To use the previous example, when a rep makes a presentation to established investors, you don't want the prospects to register surprise or shock at how good the product is. In a similar vein, the sales rep need not resort to exaggerated body language to make a point.

In a home situation, you will either record dialogue or have the talent act out a scene without any audio track at all since the narrator may have already recorded an explanation of what's happening during the studio session. To act out a scene without audio, have the sales rep read from the presentation book or use whatever props are needed to match the narrative. The director will help you with this.

Be forewarned that whenever you get two or more talent together, the chances of getting your scene in one take are slim. Many of them have worked together on other projects and know each other well, which includes playing practical jokes on each other or trying to get the others to blow their lines. After several hours of shooting, a serious scene can turn positively silly.

For a kitchen scene, I had two veteran actors play out their dialogue without an audio track. The sales rep was supposed to be talking to the prospect about his insurance needs, and I had worked with them on how the conversation should start, what questions the prospect would ask, and how the rep would answer. The scene would eventually take up about fifteen seconds of program time.

The first take started out fine:

Rep: So you see, Mr. Jones, it's important that you plan ahead, and this product can help you meet your needs.

Prospect: Sure, I understand. It sounds like it can do a lot for me.

Rep: Tell me, Mr. Jones, do you have any children?

Prospect: Oh, yes! I keep them locked up in the basement with my wife . . .

Director: Cut . . .

They had played off each other beautifully and caught us all off guard. Once we stopped laughing and started the scene again, the next take quickly veered off into a discussion of the prospect of serving time in prison. The next take had both actors talking about something unmentionable. On and on it went, with each take more bizarre than the one before as they tried to top each other.

"Guys, we can't go on like this," I said.

"There's no audio," one of them replied. "Who's going to know?"

"Someone who can read lips," I said.

It took seventeen takes before we got it right. At least, I think we got it right. To this day, whenever I think about that program, I'm still not sure what they said.

Here are some other things to do or watch for:

- Make sure that all phones are unplugged.
- Watch out for reflective surfaces. Cabinets with glass doors, windows, and mirrors do more than just reflect light. They can also pick up a reflection of the camera and crew.
- Take up a position near the camera when taping begins, and stay there. Microphones will pick up even the slightest background noise, so don't move around or flip through the script.
- Be respectful of the person's home. Most of the time home owners will leave the premises altogether or confine themselves to another area. If they need to hold up taping for few minutes while they make a call or prepare to leave the house, be patient.

SHOOTING OUTDOORS

Moving your production outdoors takes on a life all its own as you contend with the weather, the location of your scene, and the unpredictability of life going on around you.

- Be prepared for possible changes in the weather. The day may start out sunny and warm, then suddenly turn dark, cold, windy, and wet. Whenever I shot outdoors, I always brought along a jacket, sweater, and an umbrella, depending on the season.
- Let those in your company know where you'll be, and leave more time than you think you'll need for the shoot, even if you're taping only one scene.
- Bring along any visuals or props the talent will need, along with your script and production book.
- While the crew sets up, go through the scene with the director and talent. For location shots without talent, work with the director on matching the sequence to the narrative. What camera moves will be employed? Is there some action you'd like to see, like an ambulance pulling out of a hospital or business people on their way to work?
- Interruptions during taping should be anticipated. A park scene may be marred by a stray dog walking up to the talent looking for attention. A street scene can be scrapped because of car horns and people yelling "Hi, Mom!" in the background. There's not much you can do, so take your time and set up the scene again.

While I was trying to shoot the exterior of my home office, two business-men caught on to what I was doing, stopped dead in their tracks, and put on a show for me. Instead of waiting for them to move on, I approached them and asked if they wanted to be TV stars. I shot the exterior, reset the camera for a shot of the building's front entrance, and had them walk through the doors looking very serious and professional. They had a great time, and I got an extra scene which I used for another program. Take advantage of these opportunities whenever you can.

Technical Considerations

- The equipment used for outdoor locations relies on powerful battery packs or some other portable source, so there's no need to be concerned that a scene won't look as good as studio and indoor shoots that use electrical sockets.
- Field monitors, while producing high-quality pictures, are small and may be hard to see on a bright day. It may take a few playbacks to get used to them.
- The audio technician will wear a headset to maintain the integrity of the sounds recorded. If he picks up a stray noise, he'll make sure the director knows about it.
- Even though you're shooting in daylight, a scene may necessitate the use of lights, reflector boards, and silk screens to soften and add warmth to the talent. On a windy day, unfortunately, these act like sails, so you may find yourself becoming a member of the crew by holding down a board.

WHEN YOU'RE ON LOCATION

For each of the different types of locations mentioned in this chapter I've had you bring along your production book. You'll have plenty to do as it is, but when you get a moment, write down the things you've observed and what you learned along the way.

- How long did each setup take, what equipment was used, and how were technical problems solved?
- How did the director handle the session? What were your impressions of the talent?
- How did you participate in the process? Did you feel your input was important?
- Did you get a chance to try out the camera or help set lights?
- How did a particular camera angle or movement enhance the script?

By recording your thoughts, impressions, and ideas, you won't have to rely on memory alone the next time you produce a show. When your boss or manager asks what went into a location shoot, you'll be able to talk about the experience from a number of perspectives, and she'll come to see the experience as a complex coordination of technical and personal factors.

With the studio and location shoots now completed, you're halfway there. Now you'll spend the next day or two sitting through an editing session. Muster up all the concentration and attention to detail that you can, because the editing suite is where your video program will finally be born.

AT THIS STAGE OF THE PRODUCTION PROCESS YOU SHOULD

- Bring your script and production book to every location site.
- Remember to provide visuals and props for the talent.
- Get permission to shoot company departments and to use employees.
- Invite company representatives to watch a taping session.
- Act as liaison to provide good on-site relations away from the office.
- Watch and listen for problems that arise during taping.
- Dress properly for outdoor shoots.
- Expect the unexpected.

STEP 4

Post-Production

12

The Editing Process

At the end of your studio and location shoots you will have the talent's performance on one or more tapes, depending on how many takes were necessary to record the script, how many camera angles were shot, and whether your producer/director decided to shoot one or more of what is referred to as a "safety," that is, an extra take of any given scene that can be substituted should the main scene become unusable or unworkable for some reason.

Before you go into the editing suite to start putting the show together, the director will sit down and assemble a list of all the tape shot, which scenes are on which tape, and each scene's corresponding time codes. Many directors delegate time code notation to a technician as studio and location scenes are being shot; others prefer to watch all the footage later on in the comfort of their office and write down In and Out times themselves. Either way is acceptable. The whole point of breaking down every scene into time codes and writing them down is to save everyone time and money in the editing suite.

PREPARE FOR YOUR EDITING SESSION AHEAD OF TIME

The number one complaint among editors is that producers fail to show up for their sessions prepared. Instead of sitting down for a solid, eight-hour session, editors often find themselves:

Waiting for the producer to make a decision about the program

Waiting for the client to make a decision about the program

Waiting for the producer who's waiting for the client to make a decision about the program

Waiting for critical information to arrive from the client's office
Waiting

Remember this: You will be charged for editing time whether you're actually working on your program or trying to get hold of someone back at the office to answer a question. So if you want to make the best use of your editing time, keep your budget on track, and make a good impression on your editor, follow these simple guidelines:

1.   *Be early.* If your editing session begins at nine in the morning, be there at eight-thirty. This will give you time to grab some coffee, make your phone calls, and organize the day's materials.

2.   *Have the name or names of those in your office who can answer questions regarding your program.* Good production planning eliminates unnecessary calls to the office, but occasionally your director or editor will make a suggestion that may have to be cleared, like running the program's credits over a still photo of your company's charity committee. It may sound good to you, but you never know if someone on the committee is about to be replaced or has fallen out of favor with the community.

3.   *Don't forget your script, production book, and any visuals you are responsible for.* While you were in the studio and on location, you made a lot of notes, either directly on your script or in your production book. Do not leave them behind and assume the director will remember everything that went on. When the director turns to you and says, "Do you recall if we liked the first take or the third?" you'll know which one. That way you won't have to waste time looking through all the scenes, trying to decide.

Arrange your visual elements by scene and have them ready for taping. If you're working in an editing suite with an adjoining studio, and you know you'll be shooting a lot of closeups of brochures, books, tools, or other items, spread them out on a table in the studio for easy access and read ahead in the script as you edit. As the director and editor set up one scene, you can have the right visuals ready for the next.

4.   *Know what you want.* You'd think that after all the planning you did, this wouldn't be a problem. It can be. I've had editing sessions where my clients knew exactly what they wanted . . . until they saw me set up the first scene. That's when the script went out the window and every scene became a great, electronic canvas, reworked dozens of times to satisfy a sudden urge to expand the boundaries of art. All good videos have creative play built into them. Just don't overdo it.

5.   *If you have to take a break, or make an important call, keep it short.* Do not suddenly decide to run out for cigarettes or wander into another editing suite to see what other editors are up to. It sounds silly, but I've had clients

disappear on me for hours at a time, then come back and tell me they forgot they had a meeting to go to.

The only way you will not pay for editing time is if a tape machine starts smoking or a monitor blows a tube and needs to be replaced. Document all down time.

WHAT CAN I EXPECT FROM AN EDITING SESSION?

The studio shoot may have seemed slow and tedious at times, what with lighting changes and makeup breaks and that jittery camera move that spoiled an otherwise perfect take, but you were able to check off each and every paragraph of the script as it marched along to its successful conclusion.

If video production is like an army on the move, then editing is like trench warfare. Instead of ticking off whole paragraphs and pages, you'll be knee-deep in words as you wade through sentence after sentence.

Editing is a painstaking process. What was recorded with the talent merely serves as the program's foundation; what comes into play at this point is the coordination of graphic elements, music, and special effects that will turn an ordinary narrative into a multi-level performance.

The director will be able to tell you how many hours or days will be needed in the editing suite as the production date draws near. She'll have a much better idea then since most of the visual pieces will have been gathered together or worked out on paper. Keep in mind that one page of script will work out to approximately one minute of program. What you can expect in post-production is that one minute of program may take one hour or more to set up and edit.

Editing suites usually charge by the hour. If they have to provide the videotape master, music, or any special effects, you'll pay extra. These are things you'll have to discuss with the director long before you visit the suite. An editor may assume you're providing the master tape unless you tell him otherwise. If he has to prepare it for you on-site, it may take up to an hour and will be tacked on to the final bill.

Since you taped the talent in the studio, why weren't any graphic elements taped at the same time? Wouldn't it be better to go into the editing session with all the visuals, soundtrack, and special effects ready to go? The answer is no, but not because the director and the editor want to charge you as much as they can get away with. It has to do with the program's visual quality.

Every time you copy a tape onto another tape, you lose a generation; that is, you lose some of your picture quality. For purposes of your production, you will be copying scenes onto a "master" tape, which can then be copied onto VHS tapes for distribution. You want to be able to record images at the freshest possible level. Since the talent require multiple takes, it would be inefficient and expensive to have them sitting around the editing suite all day doing on-camera or voiceover narration in between the moments you're setting up an animation sequence. So you record them using high-quality tape to preserve their performance at a level that will withstand multiple copies down the line.

Graphics, on the other hand, can be set up and shot in an adjoining studio while you're editing. The image can be better manipulated and matched to the picture quality of the talent.

Let's say you need a closeup of a brochure that has fine print. If you went ahead and recorded the shot on production day, the tape would then be transferred to the master during editing and then onto VHS during duplication, a loss of two generations. That fine print will probably look like a fine blur. Shooting graphics during editing leaves you with plenty of creative space. As you begin combining words and images, you may think, "How about if we do this with the brochure instead of that?"—something you won't be able to do if you fix your shots on production day.

When you go into an editing session, you will see how these seemingly disparate elements are arranged and rearranged into a coherent whole. You will also watch every scene at least a half-dozen times as these elements are fine-tuned and tweaked, and provide input as the director and editor shape its overall look. You'll also have to pay close attention to what's happening. Many a program has run over budget during this phase of production because of indecision and carelessness.

WHAT TYPE OF PROGRAM WILL BE EDITED?

Let's review our production in terms of voiceover narration and on-camera talent.

Voiceover narrator. The talent has recorded the audio portion of the program in the studio. Several takes are required. Music and graphic elements will be added during editing.

On-camera narrator. The talent is shot in the studio. Several takes are required. Music and graphic elements will be added during editing.

On the surface these two formats look the same, with one important difference: you will have to deal with more visual elements in a voiceover program.

For an audio production, your master tape will contain a certain number of minutes of voice and nothing but voice. You must fill in the time with music and graphics to keep it moving. This is where you incorporate print material, CGs, special effects, and the other elements we discussed in Chapter 9.

For an on-camera production, your master tape will contain a certain number of minutes of on-camera narrator. Music and graphic elements may only occupy two or three minutes of the program. You could even leave your narrator up on the screen the entire time, using only the props around her to highlight key points. The program would be dull, but at least there'd be something on the screen to look at. Of course, here you also have the option of breaking up the program with graphics: closeups of a brochure, text superimposed over a contract, and video effects.

I don't particularly favor on-camera narration over an audio recording, as there are many different techniques involved and unique rules that apply to each. That choice is a collective effort that begins with the first meeting and the development of the script, and ends with the director, the editor, and yourself. As you gain experience, as you begin to watch other programs with a keener eye, your ability to decide what works best with what and when will become more focused.

IN THE EDITING SUITE

Your first trip to an editing suite will seem as alien to you as what you saw the first time you stepped into a studio control room. There you will find players, recorders, switchers, patch bays, audio boards, graphic generators, monitors, CD and tape players, turntables, and a host of other electronic toys that will somehow breathe life into the lifeless tapes you hold in your hand.

As you become acquainted with the video industry through magazines and organizations, you'll hear a lot of talk about "off-line" versus "on-line" editing and which is better for your program.

Let's cut through the arguments for a moment and set them apart. Simply put, an off-line edit is a rough cut of the program. If you worked for an advertising agency that was putting together a national campaign for a major client, an off-line edit definitely saves time and money. You have much more room to work with off-line because images can be rearranged to satisfy the client.

For our purposes an on-line—or cuts-only—edit will do just fine. Your program is simple and pre-approved. You're working from a script OK'd by management. The talent has already been selected. There are no Industrial Light and Magic-style effects to worry about. There's no reason why you can't sit down and produce a quality program in one two-day session.

This is not to say that your program is less important than a program put together by a large corporation that opted for an off-line edit. Far from it. An on-line edit is preferable because of the planning you went through during the pre-production phase and the limitations of your budget. You want to get it right the first time. There should be no surprises in the final cut.

Before you get started, here's a brief rundown on the most important equipment you'll find in an editing suite:

Players and recorders. An editing suite should have at least two 3/4-inch tape players and a master recorder. With these you can run two tapes at once and switch back and forth between the two while recording.

Switcher. As the name implies, this handy console allows the editor to switch between any video player, music device, special effect, computer graphic, and camera at any given moment. Watching an expert editor manage this wealth of visual power is like watching a conductor lead an orchestra through a Mahler symphony. It's awesome.

Computer graphics generator. Text is typed into this system and stored in "pages." You can also add effects such as checkmarks or stars and pictures, color and shade every word or letter, make text dance across the screen, or flip the screen upside down if that's what you want. Here's where you can get directly involved. If you have a list of benefits and features that need to be shown, many editors will allow you to type them into the system yourself while he prepares the next scene with the director. Give it a try. It never hurts to ask.

Audio board. You've probably seen these before on television when a show takes you inside a music recording studio. This console can have hundreds of knobs, buttons and "pots" that make ordinary sounds take on whole new characteristics. This central unit controls all audio components, from the videotape players to the turntable.

Music players. The sophistication of today's editing suite covers all music formats. Aside from a turntable you'll also find a tape deck, a CD player, and a library of music at your disposal.

One of the things you'll discover as you work with editors is that music is more than a bouncy theme shoved into a program's background to fill gaps in the narration. Music serves a purpose, and they will suggest a number of themes that will enhance your script.

Music libraries have been recorded specifically for industry use. Never use commercial music unless you've obtained copyright clearance from a publisher. You may think that no one will ever know you used that top ten song—and you may be right—but if anyone does find out and you have no legal clearance, you will lose a very expensive lawsuit. Copyright infringement is not only unlawful but unprofessional.

Monitors. You'll see lots of them. The trick is to keep in mind which monitor goes with which tape machine, camera, and computer graphic. The reason an editor needs so many monitors is to ensure the integrity of each image, whether it's playing or being recorded. If any image is to be altered, it's much easier to do so on a separate screen before the edit is made.

Digital video effects. Otherwise known as DVE, these special effects can make routine images more interesting. Examples of DVE include digitization, posterization, multiple image display, and motion control. Some studios consider their DVE capabilities standard fare; other studios charge for their use.

Edit controller. This panel oversees the videotape players and recorder. A time code keypad or search dial (akin to the rewind and fast forward buttons on a VCR) will locate the scenes you want and lock them in for the edit. Scenes can be trimmed or extended according to your needs.

That takes care of the editor's basic arsenal. Now let's talk about some of the basic features of the editing process.

CUT AND PASTE

A good editor is like a good engineer; give him a workable blueprint with workable materials and he'll work wonders.

The better prepared you are for an editing session, the faster your program will come together. This means bringing along a finished script, showing up with all the necessary flat art (brochures, flyers, etc.), and making a comprehensive list of text that needs to be entered into the computer graphics generator.

The director will be there in the suite with you when editing begins. The director will know what's on each tape and has entered time code notes into the script to help find specific scenes.

What's first? Every program begins with a master tape that has been black-burst and time coded. Don't even think about laying in any frames before this is done.

If you play a blank 3/4-inch tape on a machine, all you will see is the same kind of snow you see on television early in the morning before a station signs on. In video, this type of track is unusable and will not accept the transfer of images and sound with any reliability. The tape must be prepped with a black background and a time code track that the recorder will read during the editing process.

Sound confusing? In a way it does seem overcomplicated. After all, if I have one machine with the narrator on it and another with some graphics and a third machine that will accept both sets of images, what's with all the numbers?

Again, the answer has to do with efficiency. Time coding a tape inserts an invisible, silent tracking device that tells an editing machine exactly where a scene starts and ends.

As an editor sets up a scene to be recorded, many visual and audio elements will be used at once. Keeping all these elements together requires a method of mechanical time-keeping. Since the scene will be run several times in order to fine-tune certain elements, you don't want to leave anything to chance. Music must enter in the right place; the company logo must appear on this word. If all programs depended on the precise manual timing of a human being managing twelve different elements, the world would be full of dangerously insane editors and there would be little consistency in the programs you watch every day. Hence, all videotapes must be time coded.

Also keep in mind that the images being transferred are electronic images. If you don't like the way a scene looks, you can do it again without worrying that one of the pieces will suddenly drop out or not kick in when it's supposed to. The system will initially be set in a preview mode; the recorder will not accept any cuts until you're satisfied.

Editing can be a trying experience. You'll watch the same scene numerous times, and it will seem to take forever to record. In a way this is true. At the end of a day's editing session you may only have a few minutes worth of program recorded. There's not much you can do to speed this up. Mechanical considerations aside, you will want to make sure every scene meets with your approval.

- Are names spelled correctly and assigned to the right people?
- Are numbers and dates correct?
- When the narrator talks about a particular brochure, is that what the audience will see?

No matter what electronic wizardry the editor performs in the assembly of the show, it's up to you to point out problems. In this way you supersede the director in managing the overall look of the program. You're the proofreader who keeps an eye on accuracy. You're the diplomat who makes sure a location shot of the CEO or company owner doesn't show him smoking a cigarette or holding anything stronger than coffee. You're also the musician who decides not to put background music into a number-intensive scene. Don't figure you can sit back and let an editor and director who don't know your company call the shots. Get involved! Even if you make a suggestion that doesn't work, learn from the experience of finding out why it doesn't work.

At the same time, an editor will have his own expectations of you. He may ask how a certain scene looks to you, or he may run an idea past you that may enhance the look of the program. He may work with businesses like yours week in and week out, but to him every program presents a new set of challenges. He also wants you to get what you want.

I spent three days on one particular project laying in music for a long and complicated program requiring two dozen different selections. By Friday afternoon the house producer, editor, and I had completed most of the work, but then we hit a snag. The selection we chose for a scene came up five seconds short. We really liked the piece and didn't want to search for an alternative, so we sat back and discussed what we could do about it.

"What if we take the last six measures and repeat it?" I asked, as the piece ended with a percussion solo.

The house producer caught on to my idea immediately. "No, repeat the last ten measures."

The editor rewound the audio tape, added in another ten measures, and ran a preview of the scene again. This time the music ended at just the right moment, and there were high-fives all around. Creative spontaneity made that scene work to perfection, but it wouldn't have happened at all without one idea bouncing off another.

SO LET'S PUT IT TOGETHER!

Step one. You'll notice that an editor will not lay in a music soundtrack right away. This is because videotape can be manipulated on multiple levels, or tracks. In other words, the editor will place the narration on track number one, and later on, after all the cuts have been made, the music will be inserted on track number two.

Adding the right musical emphasis is easier once you see how the program comes across visually. Unless you have a specific musical opening in mind that can be inserted before any words are spoken, leave the music for last.

Step two. As each scene is cued up and its corresponding support graphics are prepared, the editor will use the switcher to check it and decide when and where it will make its appearance. To help ensure a smooth transition between scenes, a "tail" is left on the end of the last shot recorded; that is, the editor will let the shot run longer than is needed.

This is necessary due to the black background running throughout the tape. When you add the next scene, the tail from the previous scene provides a cushion to be taped over. Otherwise, if you try to butt two scenes together against the background, the result will either be an awkward-looking jump-cut or a second's flash of black.

Step three. The script will be pieced together word by word, line by line, and action by action. Once you've established a regular rhythm from scene to scene, you'll see how easily it comes together. While Tape #1 shows the narrator holding up a copy of the sales brochure, Studio Camera #1 is focused on your insert shot of the brochure. At the same time, the computer graphics generator is readied to list the product's benefits and features, and a few well-placed sparks of light are set to burst through the screen as if the product has a powerful life of its own.

Step four. The editor sets it up, checks to make sure the colors match, runs it a couple of times, and then turns to you.

"Does this look okay?"

And so it begins.

AT THIS STAGE OF THE POST-PRODUCTION PROCESS YOU SHOULD

- Remember to bring along any artwork, print material, your script, and production book to the edit session.
- Keep in mind that editing is a time-consuming process. Don't expect instant results.
- Familiarize yourself with the wide array of editing technology available.
- Get involved! If an edit doesn't look right or ring true, say so. Make sure all words are spelled correctly and on-camera items are properly identified.

13

It's Showtime: Making Your First Presentation

With perhaps a few bumps along the way, the program has been completed to your satisfaction. The script was well written and approved with only minor revisions, the talent captured the essence of the program and your company, the director and production crew fussed and fidgeted until every scene was worthy of an Academy Award, and the editor crafted a seamless story that will grab the audience's attention from the very first frame.

As you watch, the master is prepared and transferred to a VHS tape, a copy you now proudly tuck under your arm as you envision a triumphant return to the office. Veni, Vidi, Vici.

Welcome back to reality.

Your accomplishments are certainly worthy of at least a letter of thanks from the president of the company, but until that time you still have one last leg of the journey to complete—the final presentation for approval.

Be forewarned that presenting the video to your superiors will not be a cakewalk. If you take a lackadaisical approach to what seems like a formality, you may step into a trap that will leave you overwhelmed and emotionally drained.

KNOW YOUR AUDIENCE

After you met with your managers for the first time to discuss the project, you had some work to do. The treatment and production schedule were developed with one purpose in mind, and that was to get everyone involved in the project to work toward a common goal. It ensured cooperation and brought out the expertise and abilities of numerous personalities and departments.

When you walk into that presentation meeting, you'll bear the standard of that collective effort. All these people will want to see what you were able to make of their thoughts and desires. This will be tricky, to say the least. The persona you project must be that of diplomat, magician, and negotiator as you field questions, complaints, and demands.

SIX RULES FOR MAKING A SUCCESSFUL PRESENTATION

There are a few fast rules you should observe when making a presentation:

1. Bring along your production book. If a question should arise concerning some aspect of the program, you'll have your script, calendar, and production notes at the ready.
2. Make sure everyone watches the program at the same time and in the same room. Never let a manager or executive take a copy home so he can watch it over the weekend. Chances are he won't.
3. If your company doesn't have a VHS player and monitor, rent them from the production company or a vendor ahead of time. Do not rely on anyone else to provide them.
4. Arrange chairs in the viewing room so that everyone can comfortably watch the show and hear the words clearly.
5. When scheduling a presentation room, make sure that all potential distractions are eliminated from the area.
6. Before making the presentation, request that the first viewing be seen all the way through without comments or interruptions.

When you visit a production studio, you'll notice that it's equipped with separate viewing rooms for the clients. This attention to detail shows that the studio is serious about its projects, and that the business to be discussed is extremely important. Your presentation room should project the same image. It should say that you care about your program and your viewers. And rightly so, for it's going to be up to management to pass judgment on your work.

INTO THE LION'S DEN

Once you've managed to get everyone together, the success of your video comes down to five or ten minutes of sight and sound. And those few minutes will seem like hours.

When you watch a movie with a group of friends, you're pretty tolerant of what's presented to you on the screen unless it's truly objectionable in content or it just plain stinks. If you all agree it was pretty good, you discuss what it is you liked about it and move on. Unfortunately, corporate politics is a different animal, an unpredictable entity that can turn on you at a moment's notice. Whether it's your first project or your hundredth, your video will always be your baby, and more than one hair on your neck is likely to stiffen if someone tries to take it away from you.

Here's how it works. Everyone watches your program in silence; some take notes. After it's over, there's usually a general agreement that it looks good. There may be one or two comments about something that was done particularly well. And you'll receive some kudos for a job well done.

But you should realize that behind the smiles and cordial nods every one of your viewers is a critic. More than that, there's an underlying belief that nothing an employee does is immune to scrutiny.

Hang on. The dominant manager of the group will be the first to speak up, pointing out that the music doesn't seem appropriate at some particular place, or asking why a certain piece of information was left out. Never mind that she gave her OK to the script. Not to be outdone, the others will begin voicing their opinions. Soon, it will seem like a pack of wild dogs is circling you, nipping at you until you weaken enough for them to move in for the kill.

So on the one hand you've just been complimented for doing a fine job in so little time, and on the other you have failed to read their minds. Now that they've seen the finished product, they decide it's a good stepping stone for what they really had in mind all along.

At this last comment your hard-won lessons in video production transport you into a fantasy rebuttal wherein you clutch the script in one hand while shaking your fist at the infidels who dare speak such heresy. They are not only blind, but deaf and uncomprehending as well. None of them could possibly appreciate the artistry involved. You are insulted beyond words.

Well . . . perhaps the fantasy wouldn't go that far, but such comments will make you wonder at times what planet these people are from. After all the OKs and go-aheads, why are they only now having problems with it?

Not everyone sees what you see. You've been intimately involved with this production for two months, wondering day after day how all the work you've done will turn out. Even when you sat in on the editing session and watched the program one last time you probably marvelled at your technical accomplishments more than anything else.

Your viewers will take a very different approach. They've been waiting for The Word. They haven't seen the hours you spent in the studio working with the talent to breathe life into the script. They weren't there when you made the decision to abbreviate one of your program points because the words took up too many lines on the CG page. Your viewers weren't there, and they don't care.

Think about the movies you've seen. How many times have you been enchanted by ads for the latest blockbuster with your favorite stars and fantastic special effects, only to discover that it's a colossal bore that you can't wait to end? When the movie was over, did you commiserate with the technicians who spent months working around the clock to make that computer animation sequence look real? Did you fret that the director lost sleep bringing his troubled, tortured vision to the screen? Of course not. Someone asked you how you liked the movie, and you said it stunk. And that's about it.

Your audience will judge your video by the same emotional standards. Not by the brilliance with which you manipulated text or zoomed in on the sales kit as the music swelled to an ethereal peak, but by a simple fact: did the program accomplish its mission or not?

That's what managers and executives will be looking for when you play the tape. When it's all over with, are they going to want to share your program with others?

You're going to be the recipient of their thoughts and comments. Brush up on your diplomatic skills, because you're going to need them.

HANDLING YOUR CRITICS

Program objections can be broken down into two categories:

1. Objective criticisms
2. Subjective criticisms

Your strategy in any presentation is to break them apart, to keep them separate and at a very discreet distance from each other.

1. *Objective criticisms.*
Tackle these first because they're the easiest to identify and resolve. Objective criticisms deal with obvious mistakes:

- People, places, and things incorrectly identified
- Numbers out of sequence
- Highlights and features in the wrong order

    Example: A segment of your news program covers a regional meeting of sales managers. One of the meeting's participants is identified as John Smith from Shreveport, Louisiana when in fact it's really John Taylor from Tallahassee, Florida.

    Example: Your training video refers to a workbook, but instead you show a procedures manual.

    Example: A mathematical equation transposes key numbers: 9,384 instead of 9,834.

If you reviewed your program carefully during the planning, production, and post-production phases, such mistakes should be few, if any.

In general, these types of mistakes are easy to repair. We left open days in the production schedule to fix such problems, and the fixes can be done in a few hours. A quick call to your house producer and you'll be back in the editing suite in no time.

Fixing errors involves several scenarios:

- For the incorrectly identified sales manager, the master tape is cued to the proper place, the location tape set to the same scene, a new key is created with the right name, and the old sequence is replaced.
- For the workbook example, the master tape is cued to the proper place, the camera reset with the correct visual, and the new scene is dropped in.
- Correcting numbers depends on whether or not your editing facility saved your information to computer disk. This saves time because a page is merely called up and the number or numbers fixed. Otherwise you might have to recreate the entire page.

Not all errors are the result of lapses on your part. For one of my news shows, for example, I shot a prospecting brochure that had been developed for the Hispanic community. After I finished the last edit, the sales department called and asked if I could substitute a new and improved copy of the brochure that was about to be sent to the field. No problem. I set up a camera, attached the new brochure to a backboard, rewound the master tape to the appropriate section, and made a clean substitution.

2. *Subjective criticisms.*
These are the ones that will test your patience. Handling feelings and opinions requires subtle political gymnastics. The question is, can you take the heat?

Subjective criticisms may involve:

- Your choice in music, special effects, animation, and typefaces and colors for words and numbers
- The manner in which a scene was shot, such as using zooms, pans, and other camera movements
- The performance of your talent

Don't panic. Take their concerns one at a time. Most subjective criticisms managers have concerning a program are really not criticisms at all. Some merely reflect thinking out loud. They can live with the program, and on second thought, it's really okay. When such a comment is made, don't feel you have to answer right away. Someone else in the group may override the objection for you. Let the dynamics of group discussion work to your advantage.

If someone feels that a certain piece of information was left out of the script, point out that in the creation of the program a fundamental question was confronted: Where do you draw the line between presenting a strong case for your program and overloading the audience with too many facts and figures? To keep the program focused and the audience interested, it was necessary to present enough facts to make a point, then move on.

In the case of a new product introduction, you want your sales reps to be excited about how good the product is without having it overshadowed by page after page of legalese. A training program might refer the audience to the manual and workbook for more information. A public service program should get people involved.

Think of it this way: network news programs have a limited amount of time to give viewers an overview of a story and enough information to explain what's happening. A television ad for a new car concentrates on how safe the vehicle is or how fuel efficient it is. If either one of these situations went into every particular, imagine how incredibly long and boring it would be.

Another objection may involve your choice of music. Ask what it is exactly that bothers them. Music should accentuate; it should motivate and inspire. Do they just not like the selection? Do they think it's too loud or too soft? Since the program's music was recorded on a different track than the video portion of the script, replacing a selection can easily be done, but be sure they really want it done; otherwise you may be making multiple trips to the editing suite until you find a selection that will satisfy everyone.

The most frequent question you'll receive is why something was shot a particular way. Why was the brochure shot on an angle and not straight on? To answer, address the need for variety and to keep the imagery fresh. You have to hold the audience's attention. Shooting scenes in different ways forces viewers to think about what they're seeing. If every brochure were shot straight on, after a while they'd all start to look the same. The same goes for typefaces and colors. You want words and numbers to stand out.

Then you will be asked, "Can that scene in the office be changed so that the entire sales kit can be seen on the desk?" It depends. If the scene in question is an insert shot taped during the editing session, then yes, the entire sales kit can be set up on the desk and the sequence dropped into the master tape. If the scene involves the talent stepping back away from the desk and pointing to each piece of the kit, then a decision will have to be made. Yes, the scene can be changed, but it will require rehiring the talent, scheduling studio time to shoot and re-record the soundtrack, and setting extra dates for editing. These will add additional costs to the program.

On the whole, you'll want to stay away from making changes to all but the most obvious mistakes. Figure 13.1 provides a perfect illustration of what you and others can expect should you decide to rework substantial parts of the program.

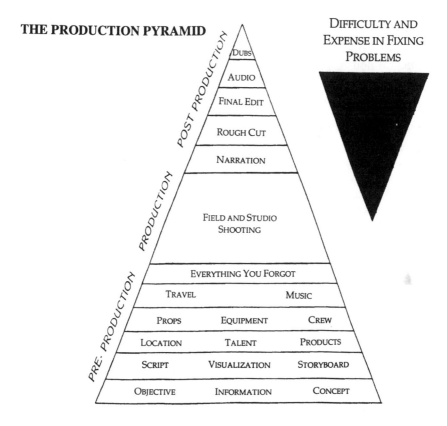

THE PRODUCTION PYRAMID

DIFFICULTY AND EXPENSE IN FIXING PROBLEMS

Figure 13.1 The Production Pyramid. Source: "Pyramid Power," by Ralph Metzner and Colleen Hartley, *Corporate Television*, September 1987

As you can see, the base of the pyramid shows how the earliest phases of production leave lots of room for shaping a program's concept and content. As the production moves on, the ability to make changes begins to narrow as time and resources become factors.

By the time you've completed a program, any major changes will require moving back down the pyramid, which leaves the program wide open to a considerable investment in production time and expense. I can tell you right now that repeated visits to the bottom of the pyramid will end any thoughts of continuing to use video as a communications tool.

So much for a discussion of program changes. After some hemming and hawing and a few huffs and puffs of mild dissent, the managers decide they like the program, so much so that they want every office to have a copy. Will that be a problem to arrange?

Always anticipate the possibility that extra copies of the program will be requested at the last moment. Since you've already discussed this with the production house, you can assure them that with their approval, you can have the master tape out today and copies back in time for distribution.

PASS ALONG SOME EXPERIENCE

Managers and executives will learn quite a bit about the video production process with every presentation you make. In theory, this should make future programs easier in terms of approvals and support. They will come to understand what it takes to put a show together, and they'll also understand that major changes are to be avoided. Most of all, they will come to understand that their input into a project is not to be taken lightly. In fact, the next script you put through for approval will be more thoroughly read and discussed.

On the negative side, your ability to produce a show will foster new and sometimes unreasonable expectations. You will be expected to create consistently good shows, no matter what the subject area or format. Minor errors may not be tolerated as easily as they once were. Unexpected delays in duplication and delivery will call your reliability into question.

Stay the course. There are production areas within your control, and there are mishaps that come with the territory. Appreciating the physical limitations of the video business keeps expectations in check. If something goes wrong during a production, get all the details and explain the problem openly and honestly to your managers. Nine times out of ten problems can be solved quickly and delays kept to a minimum.

While you're at it, keep an eye out for signs that someone really likes a particular special effect or piece of music that she wants to see or hear in every program. Managers sometimes get attached to those "neat little things" that swirl and spark across the screen. Reiterate the need to make every program stand out on its own.

AT LAST!

Everyone got what they wanted. The vice-president is happy because he made the right decision to go with the video flow, the managers are happy because their involvement contributed to the program's effectiveness, and your boss is happy because you turned out to be pretty good at this after all, and that made her look good.

As for you, you've just completed your first show. If no one takes this opportunity to say it to you, then perhaps you will allow me to say it for all of them:

You are now a Video Producer.

Congratulations!

AT THIS STAGE OF THE POST-PRODUCTION PROCESS YOU SHOULD

- Take the time to schedule and prepare a viewing room for your first presentation.
- Learn how to handle objective and subjective criticisms.
- Use the production pyramid to show how major changes to a program will have an effect on production time and cost.
- Pass along some experience. When others become aware of what it takes to produce a video, they'll know what to expect next time.
- Celebrate! Give yourself a pat on the back and treat yourself to something special. You deserve it!

14

Do It Yourself: Taking on Additional Video Responsibilities

As you gain more and more production experience you'll come to rely on a regular set of outside services. These will include scriptwriters, production houses, and duplication services. You may have to engage in hit-and-miss tactics for a while until you find someone you like, but once you do there's no reason other than an outrageous price increase or shoddy service to switch to someone else.

I want to take a slight detour from our production to talk about how taking a more active approach to video production can increase your knowledge of the business and give you greater confidence in your abilities.

Why get more involved in the process? The first time you produce a show, the production company handles all the arrangements for you. It hires the talent, arranges for studio and editing time, and contacts the duplication service.

But with experience comes confidence. Once you know what you want and how you want a video to look, you should seriously consider arranging some of these production services on your own. Contacting and meeting with service representatives will not require a great deal of your time. What will take time is a commitment on your part to study the technical side of the business and to get some hands-on experience. As we discussed in Chapter 2, the more you know about video production, the more your company will come to rely upon your knowledge and expertise. Working closely with various outside services will increase that knowledge.

Another consideration is money. When a production house arranges services for you, it does the choosing. This is not especially bad because a house is not going to pick people who don't know what they're doing. In fact, it'll probably choose from a corps of favorites that have given it good results over the years. But it may not have the time to shop around like you can if you are doing the production on your own. In choosing your own services, you can make long-term deals or take advantage of special offers you might not have known about before. More than that, you can develop some great industry friendships.

TALENT AGENCIES

This is a good place to start because talent agencies are inherently people-oriented. They represent men and women who are dedicated to their craft and to the companies they work for. If a company really likes the quality of the work, it may hire the talent exclusively for many years. Steady work from a single company doesn't come around too often in this business.

Because talent is represented by the three unions we discussed, you won't be able to negotiate on price. What you will get, however, is a vast library of photos, resumés, and demo reels to be used at your discretion, plus updates as your name is added to various mailing lists.

It may not seem like much, but having dozens of pictures and reels within arm's reach saves quite a lot of time if your next production has to be done as soon as possible. Imagine going into a meeting with enough faces and voices to get program planning off to a fast start. The convenience you provide managers and executives will show that as a producer you're already on the case.

When you call a talent agency, introduce yourself to a representative and explain the types of programs your company is interested in doing. Request the latest demo reels and photos of some of its male and female talent. While you're at it, ask about and make a note of union rates and billing.

Once you get the ball rolling, you will receive new cassettes and photos on a regular basis. How you classify the talent—by gender, corporate specialty, or personal gifts—is up to you.

Establishing a good working relationship with talent will find its way back to the agency. Other actors and actresses will court your attentions, and reps will keep your name and company on the favored list. Develop a good rapport and you'll find an agency very receptive to your needs.

SHOOT IT YOURSELF

In a previous chapter we discussed the visual elements of a video production. One of these was location footage. For this particular production, you had the production company shoot the exterior of your building and a few office scenes to add body to the script.

Once the show is completed, however, you may find that you have several months before you have to do another show. In the meantime, you've come up with all kinds of ideas for office scenes you'd like to add to the company's library. Rent the equipment and do it yourself.

Easier said than done, you say. You don't have the foggiest notion how to operate video equipment, and even if you did you're all thumbs.

Nonsense. All it takes is some basic instruction and a little confidence. Experience will take care of the rest. When you sat in on the studio shoot, you probably noticed that the technicians executed a set routine:

1. Set up tripod.
2. Attach fluid head mount for the camera.
3. Attach camera to the tripod.
4. Run cables from camera to monitor, tape deck, and power source.
5. Turn everything on.
6. White balance camera and focus picture. The white balance switch on a camera adjusts its internal eye so that colors remain true to the subject.
7. Shoot.

When you're ready to strike out on your own, you'll find that a good rental company does more than just deliver stock to your door and that the van drivers do more than just shuttle pieces back and forth. They know every-thing there is to know about the equipment they provide, how it's hooked up and turned on, and how it can be used to its best advantage. If you ask ahead of time, a delivery person can take a few minutes out to set it up for you and give you some helpful pointers.

Also, most pieces of equipment come complete with instruction manuals. No one expects you to be a genius here.

Under certain circumstances you may not even need a lighting kit, such as when you're shooting outdoors. For indoor shots, most cameras can operate in almost any type of light. They can compensate for less than ideal conditions and still give you a good picture. As long as the quality is good and you are able to shoot the necessary action or scene, that's all that matters. As time goes on you'll be able to experiment with your environment by adding lights and filters.

For shooting around the office all you need is a camera, a tape deck, a portable monitor to see what you're doing, and tape. One 60-minute tape can give you dozens of scenes. An umbrella light (a small light source on a stand with an umbrella attachment for intensifying or softening its beam) will illuminate a background and eliminate pesky shadows.

Renting equipment pays for itself. With a library of office scenes at your disposal you can cut production time and cost. Never discount the opportunity to tape an event, a procedure, or a department. You never know when it will come in handy.

Okay, so you'll give it a try. You'll get a referral from the production house, make some calls, and start shooting. Pretty easy, right?

In many ways the video business is transactional, an exchange of money for a service. But if you look close enough and turn over a few stones, you'll find there's so much more.

LET'S MAKE A DEAL

The first time you rent equipment on your own, a rental company is going to play your production needs by the book. You'll place an order, the company will deliver it, and you'll pay for it. The price you see in a catalog or are told over the phone is what you'll get.

What a lot of first-time producers don't understand is that cut-and-dried transactions don't necessarily have to remain so. All it takes is a desire to get to know who you're dealing with and what that person can do for you.

The video industry is extremely dynamic and in a constant state of flux. It is an industry populated with creative men and women who would like nothing more than to be considered the best in their area of expertise. People with low standards and lack of drive don't last very long, and those who have been tagged for providing poor service are well known. There may be many business markets out there, but there are very few places to hide.

When you talk to a rep, whether that person deals with videotape or high-tech equipment, you're dealing with a professional who has more experience than you might realize. Many of them are producers, camera persons, artists and musicians, among other things. And what they can do for you is largely a matter of how far you want to take it.

Cultivate these contacts lovingly. Many doors will open for you, and you'll make powerful allies.

Among other things, you'll often be invited to after-hour activities at their facilities. A lot of heavy hitters in the industry attend these events, people who are willing to talk to you about your business. If you want to know what's going on in the industry, or who can do what for you in the future, this is where a lot of deals are made, more so than at an organization's meeting. It's a great way to make contacts.

Your contacts will put you on regular mailing lists. You'll receive advertisements, demo reels, samples, updated price lists and catalogs, and special deals. These will often be followed up with phone calls from reps who will want to come in and show you the latest equipment.

If you become a regular and valued customer, you'll often find list prices falling by the wayside. The company may be running a extraordinary deal on a new and unlisted product. It may rent you a camera and deck for an extra day without charge. It might even let you take some equipment on a test drive to get your opinion. There are many other perks you can get if you take an active interest.

The best equipment vendor I ever worked with knew how to keep my business. On one occasion I called to rent a teleprompter and mentioned that I was also looking for a machine to transfer some slides to videotape. I didn't need the machine for that particular production, but the rep told me that the company had just received a new slide-to-tape system and was eager to have someone try it out. I got to use the machine free for a week, and I wound up transferring numerous trays of slides and images that I was able to use in other productions. All I had to do was make my needs known, and the rep did the rest.

Your responsibility to a relationship like this is loyalty. Companies want your business—and will do whatever it takes to keep it—but they won't take you very seriously if you take unfair advantage of them. Your company's reputation can get around the industry very quickly, too.

I knew a communications manager who serves as a perfect example. He would bring in a rental rep and go over her catalog and price lists with her. If a project was coming up, he would contract with the rep to get a special first-time deal. This manager was a poor planner, so he would usually put in his order two days before a shoot. Since the rep's rental stock was generally unavailable on such short notice, she would run around like crazy trying to meet the manager's demands.

At some cost to the rental company, the rep would deliver as promised and even cut the rental price. The manager got his equipment inexpensively—which made his budget look good—and after the program was completed, he would move on to another rental company and whatever deal he could get from it for the next project.

Needless to say, his reputation in the local industry became legend. The manager was still able to get people to work for him, but they were now wary of doing anything more than they had to for him and the company.

TRADE SHOWS

A moment ago I mentioned that vendors will often invite you to visit their facilities to check out their latest equipment and services. The same holds true for trade shows, many of them sponsored by local studios and other video-oriented companies.

Trade shows present a wonderful opportunity to meet with dozens of manufacturers. Aside from picking up their latest catalogs and brochures, you'll also be able to try out their wares. You'll get to try out their newest cameras, editing equipment, and even sophisticated paintbox modules.

Don't worry about not knowing what to do. The company rep will gladly give you a demonstration, then turn the equipment over to you to show you how user-friendly it is.

COMPANY SUPPORT

At the start of the show you were a company employee assigned to produce a video for your vice-president. You had no idea where to start, you were unaware that such a wide range of services existed, and you had no concept of what went into production and post-production.

You've changed, haven't you? Some of the darker corners of the industry have since been illuminated, you know some of the lingo, and you're getting a good feel for the inner workings, rhythms, and techniques of the business.

I bring this up because at some point you will have to justify taking on portions of video production yourself. You may not receive objections in the way of flat-out refusals to rent equipment and otherwise spend company money, but some manager or executive not associated with your projects may wonder where all of this is leading. This is not exactly in your job description.

Video is not an easy concept to explain. Yes, it does appear that you're spending a lot of money to make a tape that will sit on a shelf waiting to be used at some undetermined time. Why do it if you're not going to use it right now? Why contract for services on your own when a production company can do it for you?

Shooting office scenes on your own is less understandable than having a production company do it for a specific show, but the results are nevertheless important. The success of any corporate video is derived in part from the support it receives from its viewers. That support begins with the part-time help in the mail room and extends well beyond the boardroom.

I wrote and produced several types of programs for a company that was making its first commitment to video. The department I worked for wanted its sales offices—all seventy-five of them—to stay informed and motivated.

At first I had a difficult time scheduling people to appear on-camera for interviews and stories, and sometimes the information I requested took weeks to find its way to me. A few of the regional vice-presidents were reluctant to give me their time, unsure about being associated with the new medium. They were convinced that memos were the only way to go.

After the first couple of shows, I began to see a difference in the way they approached video. The executives began to fight over what the next program would be about, who would provide the information, and who would be in it. After that, there was never any shortage of program material. In fact, I had to practically bar the doors of the studio to keep them out. Was it because they had suddenly discovered their true calling as TV stars? No. The reason was that the field offices responded enthusiastically to the shows. Everyone watched them and sent in comments and ideas. Some people sent their own videotapes, photographs, slides, and sales tips. With that kind of popularity, the previously reluctant vice-presidents quickly jumped on the bandwagon. No one wanted to be left out of the process.

The managers soon stopped thinking about video in terms of money and instead started thinking of it as a means of sharing a common purpose with their charges. They also started thinking about new ways of using video, particularly for education, training, and executive messages. Video wasn't so mysterious or scary anymore. It was accessible and capable of many things.

As I said, all this is difficult to convey if you've ever been confronted with the question of why you're spending company money on video when you're not doing a show. In that case, let the programs you produce and the images you capture tell the story. And welcome their support, even if given grudgingly.

YOUR FUTURE AS A VIDEO PRODUCER

The assistance you receive from vendors will add depth and strength to your abilities as a producer. Who knows—you might even develop a taste for writing and directing.

Through vendors you will become acquainted and familiar with just about every facet of video equipment and production techniques. Combining this knowledge with what you learn from association meetings, magazines, demo reels, and other sources, the next time a house producer wanders off into technobabble or tries to impress you with fancy features, you'll have firm ground to stand on.

A natural by-product of what you learn will be a leaner, more efficient production. You'll get exactly what you want. Video will no longer be a mystery; in fact, mystery will soon turn to mastery.

AT THIS STAGE OF THE POST-PRODUCTION PROCESS YOU SHOULD

- Work with rental services and talent agencies to help establish personal and company rapport and to build a library of information you can use for future productions.
- Consider shooting your own location scenes.
- Attend trade shows and tours of production and post-production facilities to learn about the latest video technology and services.
- Cultivate company support for your efforts.

15

Video Politics

You can't escape it. No matter what you say or do in this day and age, chances are you will offend someone. That racy joke you heard at lunch may have seemed funny at the time, but would you repeat it to someone you didn't know very well? How would you feel if you were reduced to a stereotype for the sake of someone else's amusement?

For all of the attention given to political correctness in our schools, places of business, and government, sexism and racism still play a significant role in the images we see on a daily basis. Some of them are subtle, social shadings on the part of advertising agencies and television executives, who use demographics as a way of justifying their shows and campaigns. Others are more blatant, using fear and misunderstanding to perpetuate public opinion.

When you produce a video for your company or organization, you're doing more than just "getting the word out." You're telling your audience who you are, what your company represents, and what it thinks about its employees and its customers. And like that joke you heard at lunch, there are some things that should never find their way into your programs.

Why devote a chapter to video politics? When productions are brought in-house, or when a company assumes greater control over the shows it produces, good taste is often left outside the back door. What begins as a simple comment during a planning meeting, a comment that starts, "Wouldn't it be funny if we did this?" can easily turn into an unwarranted and unintended assault on a person or persons not considered by those in the meeting. Even though the comment may be based on an actual experience, putting it on video magnifies the experience a hundred-fold and is likely to bring about nothing but trouble for your organization. Your job as a producer is to recognize the warning signs that can make your productions the target of protests.

173

WHERE DO MISCONCEPTIONS COME FROM?

To understand why we do and think the things we do, we first need to understand the ways in which we are bombarded by the media. Here are some examples of the subtle and not-so-subtle messages we see and hear:

- Why are all major televised sporting events announced by men? Statistics clearly show that women are just as interested in sports as men, and are just as knowledgeable. The next time you watch sports on television, look at the crowd. Are there no women available who could call a baseball or football game?
- Why do cleaning commercials feature women? Are advertisers telling us that men have no interest in keeping their homes, clothes, and children clean? For that matter, why are tool commercials male-dominated? Certainly in a society with many single women and mothers, the thought of taking on household repair projects must have occurred to them at some point.
- When was the last time you saw a mainstream movie where the heroine wasn't a screaming, clutching victim? When was the last time a man didn't have to resort to violence to solve a problem?
- In their search for realistic stories of the street, why do television shows portray minorities as gang-affiliated, gun-toting psychopaths?
- For all of the network talk about ethics, why have we seen a proliferation of news magazines covering lurid sex stories? Why is there a preoccupation with gossip and innuendo?
- Why do print advertisers need to portray nudity in order to sell a product?

THE WORST OF THE WORST

The most blatant print ad I've ever seen was a liquor ad in which a half-empty bottle of bourbon was broken down into major events in the drinker's life. The boss calling him by his first name was worthy of a glass, as was the great deal he got from an antique dealer for a piece of second-hand junk he had purchased at an unpainted furniture store. But when his wife leaves the cap off the bottle, resulting in the evaporation of his precious liquor, the last event reads "Sign Divorce Papers." What a heartwarming message.

The worst television commercial ever produced hit the airwaves some years ago and died a quick death due to public outrage. It was a beer commercial in which the featured characters implied that they would hurt the viewers if they didn't buy the product. It sure made me want to run out and get some.

On a local level, the worst commercial ever aired in the Chicago area was produced by a swimming pool company. Instead of showing families enjoying a well-constructed and safe backyard pool, the viewer was treated to the sight of an overly endowed woman in various closeups diving, swimming, and finally toweling herself off, with particular attention paid to certain parts of her body. As I recall, the commercial was shown twice before it was pulled. The station's switchboard must have lit up like a Christmas tree. The amazing thing about this commercial was not that it was aired at all, but that it was aired during a local five o'clock newscast, not during a late-night show.

HOW DOES THIS APPLY TO CORPORATE VIDEO?

Unfortunately, I've seen too many video programs over the years that took their cue from television and movies by establishing their own stereotypes of office workers, the people who manage them, and the people they serve. Among them:

- The crazed, maniacal boss who yells at everyone
- The cowering underling
- The blond-haired, bubbleheaded secretary
- The vixen
- The pompous know-it-all
- The sports nut
- The burned-out sales rep
- The demanding client from hell

I'm sure these character studies seemed appropriate when discussed during pre-production, but the results were inevitably embarrassing. You'd be amazed at the number of programs out there that rely on these and other stereotypes, and yet there doesn't seem to be any end in sight.

I'm at a loss to explain why these images keep cropping up. Yes, there are Type A bosses who explode at every little thing, and there are clients who expect perfection, but these are the exceptions. Human nature is too complicated to explain in terms of one trait or one action, especially when it's applied to one gender or race. Whenever someone says it would be funny to show a secretary agonizing over a broken nail while three clients are on hold, or suggests that you show a minority waiting in line at the welfare office, stop that thought before it gets out of hand. Get back to the purpose of your program, and stay there.

WHAT'S RIGHT AND WHAT'S WRONG?

With all of the attention being paid to correcting social injustices in our society, the first thought that goes through any producer's mind is what she can't say or do. Will her program be boring if she sticks to the straight guidelines of propriety?

No program should be dull. Yes, there are some things you shouldn't even consider putting in a video no matter how funny or pertinent they may seem to be, but that doesn't mean you can't be effective and interesting with your subject matter.

When I was producing a variety of videos for an insurance company, I adhered to certain strict policies no matter what type of program I was producing:

1. No one holding a cigarette or a drink during a meeting breakout or social gathering was ever taped.
2. Equal time was given to both men and women, of all races, backgrounds, and levels of success.
3. Regional vice-presidents and managers were always seen interacting with their people.
4. Enthusiasm and action were key elements of any scene.

How does this translate into your own situation? Keep these guidelines in mind:

- Always show your company or organization in its best possible light. You want to show dedicated, hardworking people who believe in what they're doing.
- When designing a program concerning social issues, provide balance at all times, even when showing powerful images that may be the exception and not the rule.
- People have emotions. Let their personal stories make a case for your subject matter and provide meaningful dissent.
- Be hopeful. Not every problem has a solution, but perhaps one can be found as long as people keep trying.

USING HUMOR

Humor is a powerful tool often abused by writers and producers who think that making fun of someone or a group of people will help get the point across. Unfortunately, what starts out as an innocuous joke during a meeting can often become downright insulting to someone who may not be in on the joke, no matter how long that person has worked for the company.

I saw a video in which a company president was seen speeding away from one meeting to another in his very expensive sports car. Seems innocent enough. But at the time the video was produced the company was going through some tough times, and the sight of the company president revelling in conspicuous consumption left many in the audience snorting in disbelief, as if the president's wealth was more important than where the company was going. Needless to say, the program did not go over very well.

In contrast, another video followed a gas company employee on his way to make a slide presentation. He had never been to the meeting site before, and had to consult a hand-drawn map that looked more like an astronomical chart than a coherent set of directions. After literally driving around in circles on a country road, the employee finally made it to the meeting site, where he furiously and conscientiously set up all of his equipment only to discover that his only extension cord was two inches short of the wall socket.

What's the difference in these two approaches? For the gas company video, the humor was allowed to evolve from a situation that everyone had experienced at one time or another. The employee wasn't dim-witted or a bad employee; he had only forgotten to bring an extra extension cord.

An unproduced video script I wrote years ago used the same approach. A sales rep awoke to a picture-perfect day, and as he went through his day making sales calls he found his prospects to be friendly, cooperative, and willing to buy his product. It was the best day of his career.

Until he woke up from his dream. The day was rainy and awful, traffic was backed up no matter where he went, and he was late for all of his sales calls. Prospects slammed doors in his face or had no time to see him, and one prospect even tore up his business card. It was the worst day of his life. Again, the humor in this program was allowed to come from a situation that the audience could understand. Who hasn't had a bad day?

The most important factor to consider in any production is people. In the 1980s there was a proliferation of commercials that used high-tech animation and special effects to sell products, but they were eventually dropped in favor of a personal touch. Why? Because people sell products, and people sell ideas and concepts better than any computer-generated model could. The viewing audience had been dazzled at first, but then grew bored.

What lesson does this teach? Keep It Simple. The most efficient way of doing things is not always with great flourish. Common experience and understanding will do more for your programs than hip political humor and pop psychology. Stick to the basics, show your audience the respect it deserves, and you'll never go wrong.

AT THIS STAGE OF THE POST-PRODUCTION PROCESS YOU SHOULD

- Recognize the sexist and racist stereotypes permeating the images you see on a daily basis.
- Approach your video with fairness. Everyone has a part to play in your company's success.
- Provide balance. There are numerous sides to every issue.
- Allow humor to come from common experience.

16

Budget Videomaking

Having a production company arrange and coordinate the talent and technical aspects of your videos is a convenience worth taking advantage of, but that doesn't mean your company or organization has to shell out fifteen to twenty thousand dollars every time you're asked to produce a show. Just the opposite. Once you become familiar with all of the services offered by the video industry, you'll find that producing high-quality, budget-minded programs is nothing more than knowing where you can cut costs and how to locate the services that will help you achieve your goals.

One of the challenges you'll have to face, however, is dealing with the negative connotations associated with the concept of being budget-conscious. Even with all of the cost-cutting measures that defined the American business landscape in the late 1980s and early 1990s, there are still those managers and executives who believe that they have to spend a lot of money to create good video programs. Mention the fact that you can produce a show on a smaller budget and they think "cheap" or "inferior." Obviously, this will take some selling on your part. It means taking on a greater role in the production process and showing that the company's needs can be met without sacrificing the program's effectiveness.

In this chapter we'll look at five areas where you can hold the line on your production costs:

1. Scriptwriting
2. Talent
3. Production
4. Editing
5. Duplication

In addition, we'll look at other ways you can save money by using the resources available to you in creative ways, and set up a sample program to illustrate how a seventeen thousand dollar budget can be cut to under nine thousand dollars.

SCRIPTWRITING

The writing profession is not easy to define without looking at the background and experience of the individual. One freelancer I know of charged a company $25,000 just to be on retainer for a month's time, and collected the money for doing nothing. Another writer with many clients makes an effort to keep her billing competitive, opting for a greater number of clients to ensure long-term profitability. Yet another tends to cater to a smaller clientele within a specific industry but at a higher cost.

Aside from requesting sample scripts from the writers you find in video source guides and professional organizations, ask your house producer for a list of freelance writers she uses on a consistent basis and how much they charge. Call on a business within your industry and do the same. The more scripts you request, the easier it becomes to tell which writers were genuinely interested in their subject matter and which ones resorted to snappy catch phrases and clichés to fill script pages. You'll also be able to tell whose services are overpriced. Two scriptwriters of comparable talent—one charging $200 a page and one charging $300 a page—can translate into a difference of $500 for a five-minute program and $1,000 for a ten-minute program.

TALENT

Not all talent are affiliated with a union, and there's no law preventing talent agencies, production companies or others from representing or hiring them. I've used non-union talent for numerous shows, and some production houses use them exclusively.

Start with your video source guide and locate those agencies representing non-union talent. Ask for headshots, resumés, and demo reels. You'll see that their range of experience is no different from anyone associated with a union, and in many cases they may even specialize in working with companies like yours. Start a file, and have this information ready for your next production.

Hiring talent on your own adds a new level of responsibility to your role as a producer. It will be up to you to hire the talent directly, get a script to them, talk to them about the program, make sure they bring along an appropriate wardrobe, and confirm shooting dates and times. Keep this in mind when developing your production schedule.

The savings can be significant. Whereas you'll pay up to $1,000 per day for union talent, using non-union talent costs about $600 per day. There are even those who charge as little as $300 per day. On the surface this doesn't seem like such a big savings, but remember that the more talent you use, and the greater number of days the talent will be needed, the higher the cost. Hiring a union narrator for one studio day and three union role-play actors for one location day will cost you $4,000. Using the same number of non-union talent for the same number of days will cost $2,400.

PRODUCTION

For your first project you used a production company that hired the talent for you, along with arranging studio, location, editing, and duplication time. But if you want to cut production costs, here's where you can really make a difference in your budget by separating the actual time spent shooting your script from all other production considerations.

In an earlier chapter on hiring and working with a production company, I broke down production company services into three categories:

- Companies with in-house facilities and full-service capabilities, from concept and scriptwriting to editing and duplication
- Companies with basic in-house facilities such as a studio, but which contract out for scripting, editing, and duplication elsewhere
- Companies that have no in-house facilities, preferring to hire out some or all production services on a per-job basis

Companies in the last category are particularly well suited to the budget-minded producer, because they provide 1- and 2-person camera crews capable of shooting in three-quarter-inch, Betacam, or Super VHS, depending on your needs. Because they're small-staffed and have concentrated on one aspect of production, their prices are very reasonable.

Check your creative directory for listings under the heading Production Services. What you're looking for is a subheading something like Cameramen/Assistants, and an ad that reads something like this:

"Cost-effective freelance production services, providing 3/4-inch and Super VHS camera crews for all business applications, specializing in corporate communications and training. We have the experience and the versatility to meet your needs."

If you can't find the crew you're looking for in a source book, contact a local television station. The people there can help put you in contact with a crew or make their own services available. I've used television crews and found them to be just as good as any production company.

Television crews are great for location work. For a news program I needed to interview an office manager in Harlingen, Texas. Rather than have a camera and deck shipped all the way from Chicago, I hired a Harlingen TV crew, flew down, and we shot the necessary scenes in an afternoon. The savings kept the production on budget. I did the same when covering sales conferences in Washington, DC and Toronto.

What you'll get for your money is a professional crew that has the flexibility of working around your production schedule and the equipment to give you the look you want. What you won't get is a lot in the way of pre-production. That is, the director will expect you to provide the location, talent, and props. Even though he'll certainly help you make on-site decisions, visualizing the script is something you'll have to do on your own.

A 2-person crew working in 3/4-inch for one full day starts at around $700. Compare this with a production company that charges $2,000 a day, and managing a greater portion of your videos begins to make sense.

EDITING

Editing suites are as different as the companies that use them. Some are extremely sophisticated, offering state-of-the-art technology, some have made a limited investment in the latest tape decks and imaging software, and still others have a basic setup capable of handling on-line (or cuts-only) projects with a minimum of bells and whistles. Where can you find the best post-production value for your money? Consider contacting one of the following:

- Hospitals
- Universities
- Other companies
- Tape duplicators
- Retail stores

In other words, you're not limited to choosing an editing facility within the video industry itself. Many hospitals, universities, and companies have their own in-house studios and will provide the personnel to put your show together. Tape duplicators often advertise editing services. Retail stores are no less effective. On several occasions, I used a facility in a furniture store. It produced its own local commercials and had its studio tucked away in a corner of the showroom. Should you hire a production crew, ask if the same people provide editing services, as well.

Costs vary. A production crew service may charge as little as $50 an hour, while a retail store may quote a price of $100 an hour, still a far cry from the $250–$300 an hour you'll pay at a post-production facility listed in a creative directory. At the low end, two days of editing—16 hours—at $50 an hour will run $800. At $250 an hour, the same edit will cost $4,000.

The down side to hiring an editing facility on your own is one of experience. If you're working with a production crew that has its own editing suite, you'll have the advantage of having the director there with you to help locate the right scenes and to add additional visual elements. This is not always the case if you use another facility. You'll have to mark up your script scenes by tape number and time code (although the director can assist you with this), map out when you'll need a character generator to create words and numbers, and determine when you'll need to shoot a brochure or contract as an insert. So when you contact an editing facility, make sure that it can provide more than just tape decks and monitors. Make sure it has a character generator, a copystand or adjoining studio for insert shots, a camera, and a music library.

DUPLICATION

Duplicators charge about the same no matter where you go. A fifteen-minute program, for example, may cost $15 for 1–4 copies, $10 for 5–50 copies, and $7 for 51–100 copies. As with any service, check the quality of the duplicator's work, turnaround time, and shipping costs.

The key to saving money in duplication is not so much the difference in cost per tape from one company to another, but the number of copies you actually need. Get an exact number, including managers and executives who want their own copies, and add three to five extra tapes for the total. That way you'll cover your immediate needs and have some on hand in the event other departments want to watch the program, the company resource center wants a copy for its files, or you're asked to send a copy to someone outside the company. Adding on twenty or thirty extra copies will result in a bookcase stockpiled with tapes nobody needs, and add up to $300 in production costs.

GET CREATIVE BY MAXIMIZING AVAILABLE RESOURCES

Not every production requires that you shoot in a studio, home, or another company. In fact, if you look around at your own place of business, you can find a wealth of locations that will serve any part of your script without your ever leaving the building.

I wrote and produced an in-house program for a company training department on the benefits of office ergonomics. Throughout the course of the 12-minute program, the audience saw:

- The home office building
- The company history room
- A computer training lab

- The resource center
- Company departments

The audience also heard interviews with doctors and scientists on the proper way to monitor working conditions and make improvements in office comfort.

Rather than giving the program the big-budget look and feel of discussing ergonomics with leading experts in the field and shooting in companies on the cutting edge of ergonomic design and implementation, I received permission from the producers of a previously released program on the subject to use their interviews with the doctors and scientists, shot around the company to show ergonomics in action, hired non-union talent to act as a narrator, and wrote the script in such a way as to bring all these elements together. The total cost of the program: less than $3,000.

Okay, so I produced this program back in the mid-1980s, but the message is still the same: you don't always have to look very far to make your programs work effectively on a visual level.

Think about some areas in your place of business that can be used for your programs:

- Boardroom
- Library
- Executive office
- Cafeteria
- Loading dock
- Print services
- Training room
- Hallways
- Company grounds or garden
- Statues and sculptures

Then consider how one location can be used for two or three separate scenes. For example, let's say you're shooting a program on sexual harassment in the workplace. You could have the narrator introduce the subject from a studio setting, explain what defines sexual harassment, then show some role plays shot around the company to illustrate your points. Figure one day of studio taping for the narrator, and one location day for role playing.

Instead of shooting in multiple locations, bring your entire production in-house. To show how management must get involved in the responsibility of ensuring a safe working environment for all, shoot the narrator walking through a boardroom or standing in an executive's office. Use another office for one role play, the library or cafeteria for another. Interview a human resources representative or lawyer on company policy. Find a meeting room with tables, bookcases, and a hallway and you need only move the camera a few feet to simulate a variety of situations.

Pre-Recorded Programs

Obtaining permission to use portions of previously produced programs is not as difficult as you might think. National organizations routinely produce tapes on a wide variety of subjects. For a credit in your show or for a small fee, they're more than willing to have their work passed on to another audience, especially if your company is in the same industry. To them, it's a matter of getting the word out and reaching a greater number of people.

Check with your human resources department, training department, or company library; these departments often receive catalogs and direct mail pieces announcing the latest video programs. Contact the organization directly, explain the type of video you're producing, and ask to use those portions of its program that pertain to your script.

Information Kits

How many times have you seen posters in businesses and schools with messages ranging from the dangers of drug and alcohol abuse to workplace safety? Those posters had to come from somewhere. Government agencies and national organizations create and distribute these messages for everyone's benefit, and they can be obtained simply by writing or calling. Again, you can check with your own company to see if they are already in stock. The company may also have information packets on exercise and health, travel tips, and first aid.

In addition to enhancing your set, they may also contain the latest statistics, which you can incorporate into your computer graphics, and charts, which you can shoot as insert shots.

Historical Archives

One company I worked for had not only a company history room but a special storage area where documents, photos, sales pieces, plaques, audio recordings, models, and curios were kept. If your program needs a little historical perspective, you may find what you're looking for without using a film archive service.

These are just some of the ways you can use your company to give your shows a sense of realism and immediacy while keeping studio and remote location time to a minimum. Look around. You might be surprised at what you find.

If you want to know how independent filmmakers manage to get the most from their money, I highly recommend that you read *How I Made a Hundred Movies in Hollywood and Never Lost a Dime* by Roger Corman. The director of such low-budget classics as *The Little Shop of Horrors* (shot in two days) and *It Conquered the World,* Corman spins one tale after another as he explains how he used the same set for more than one movie, created a sea monster using a hand puppet and a fishtank, and how he managed to keep the Hell's Angels motorcycle gang under control. It's a refreshing look at overcoming obstacles and coming up with creative ways to keep a production on track and on budget from the master of the B-movie.

THE BENEFITS OF BUDGET VIDEOMAKING

For the purposes of this illustration, let's create a program and assume that a production company will handle all our needs:

Program length: 10 minutes

Program content: Company ABC's new water conditioning system; narrator to explain how the new system works, actors to demonstrate a presentation

Purpose: to train sales reps on effective presentation techniques

Shooting requirements: 1 day studio taping for narrator, 1 day location taping for actors

Editing requirements: 3 days

Talent: 1 on-camera narrator for 1 studio day, 3 actors (1 salesperson and 2 prospects) for 1 location day

Number of program copies needed: 50

Pre-production and production services

Scriptwriter

Production company

Talent

Post-production services

Editing and duplication

Based on a projected cost of these services as outlined earlier in this chapter, define your standard production costs:

Scriptwriter: $300 per page

Production company: $2,000 per day

Talent: $1,000 per day per union talent

Editing: $250 per hour

Duplication: $10 per tape

Now add your total production costs:

Scriptwriter: 10-minute script at $300 per page—$3,000
Production company: 1 day studio, 1 day location—$4,000
Talent: $1,000 per person for one day each for 4 talent—$4,000
Editing: $2,000 per eight-hour day for 3 days—$6,000
Duplication: 50 tapes at $10 per tape—$500
Total production cost: $17,500
Cost per minute: $1,750

Compare this with our cost-cutting budget:

Scriptwriter: 10-minute script at $200 per page—$2,000
Production: 2-day shoot at $700 a day—$1,400
Talent: $600 per person for one day each for 4 non-union talent—$2,400
Editing: $600 per eight-hour day for 3 days—$1,800
Duplication: 50 tapes at $10 per tape—$500
Total production cost: $8,100
Cost per minute: $810

Assuming that the company has a showroom with at least one working model of the new system and a couple of sales offices, all scenes are shot in-house. If the script calls for an in-home presentation, a company employee's living room is used.

The benefits of locating and hiring production and post-production services on your own can make a significant difference to your video budget, but keep in mind that it's not always practical or convenient to do so. There are certain types of programs, shows that contain complex technical elements or have unusual requirements, such as aerial photography, that are best served by the knowledge and expertise of a production company. You may not have the time to coordinate these services on your own, either. What you have to do is judge each program on its own merits and decide whether you can take on the responsibility of producing the entire program yourself or should share the responsibility with a house producer.

AT THIS STAGE OF THE POST-PRODUCTION PROCESS YOU SHOULD

- Consider taking on more responsibility as a producer by hiring production and post-production services on your own.

- Learn where and how you can cut your video budget in the areas of scripting, talent, production, editing, and duplication.
- Maximize the resources available to you within your own company or organization.
- Determine what types of programs you can produce on your own.

17

What Now?

Your newly established reputation as a producer and video expert will undoubtedly open new avenues for you within your company or organization. While most will be beneficial to your job and career, there are others that will seem more of a curse than a blessing.

First the good news. Having experienced the entire video production process firsthand, you will become the person to talk to when questions arise. How long will it take to produce a news program? How much will it cost for me to have some tapes copied for a training class? Can I listen to or watch some of the demo reels you have?

Your reputation will work its way through many departments, too. If your company has a library or information resource center, you may be asked to recommend worthy video publications and programs. If you regularly receive letters, ads, and other materials from production companies, you may be asked to start a routing list so others can keep up with the industry, too.

In all, your knowledge and experience will help others solve communication problems and consider alternative ways to instruct, inform, and motivate people. If nothing else, your accomplishments will have a positive effect on your next performance review.

Now for the bad news. Bolstered by the success and enthusiastic response to your program, management will see video as the be-all and end-all of company communications. Before you know it, everything from the company's quarterly report to a two-line interoffice memo will be considered perfect for production.

Instead of carefully charting the course of future productions, managers will bring you six-hour home videos of their daughters' weddings that they want duplicated for all the relatives ("You can get a deal for fifty or sixty copies, can't you?"), and newly educated experts will demand to see computer-designed, motion-controlled animation sequences, just like the stuff they saw on television last week ("What do you mean it's going to cost $300,000 for ten seconds' worth of dancing policies?").

Whatever you do, keep a low and respectable profile, because the genie is out of the bottle.

As I mentioned early on, there are many fine guides that provide useful advice on the proper use of video and when it's best to work with other media. The communications landscape is much too vast to cover in a single volume, so bear in mind that the boundaries are sometimes fuzzy and open to individual interpretation.

Get to know video's boundaries well. Make the medium serve the interests of your company, its products, its employees, and its customers. You want to provide effective communication, but you don't want to abuse it to the point of financial ruin.

THE TOP 5 ALL-TIME BAD VIDEO PROGRAMS

It won't take long for you to discover that there are a lot of bad video programs out there, programs that should never have left the meeting room or the drawing board. You'll know them when you see them, but here are a few road signs for you:

1. *The Employee Update Video.* This falls under the "Hey! Let's set up a monitor outside the cafeteria and play a tape of what's going on in the company this week" school of communications. Bulletin board postings and memos are a lot less expensive and are just as effective.
2. *The Who Needs Professional Talent? Video.* Employee and managerial involvement is fine, but . . . when . . . the talent . . . reads . . . like this, eyes following the teleprompter script with that glazed, hypnotized look, it's time to think about calling an agency.
3. *The Company Comedy Hour Video.* I'm all for humor, but I've seen some shows that were downright embarrassing. Humor is subjective at best; what's funny to some is insulting to others. Jokes and puns at company expense can get out of hand very quickly. Keep a lid on it.
4. *The Steven Spielberg Extravaganza Video.* One of my personal favorites. This is where someone takes a simple concept and turns it into a multi-media tour-de-force. Pull the reins in and keep the bells and whistles to a minimum.
5. *The Let's See Where We Can Go with This Video.* This program starts out talking about sales commissions and ends up announcing the vice-president's retirement plans after next month's country club party. A solid strategy was obviously not on the production agenda.

These may sound like a hoot to watch, but it doesn't take much for viewers to become jaded. Once you remove any incentive for an audience to think, feel, or experience something, the only thing that remains is an audience trained to sit in front of a video monitor once a week.

WHY VIDEO IS EXPENDABLE

Many communications departments have lost their funding for a number of reasons. Whether because the company as a whole lost money—necessitating the removal of support areas—or because the company was bought out by someone who already has a communications department, the video producer walks a tightrope in today's corporate environment. This is a fact of life that you will read and hear about quite often in professional circles.

Most of the time you'll hear about cutbacks; what you won't hear about are companies that dropped video because of poor planning, wasteful production practices, and a lack of favorable results for the company. You can talk about professionalism all you want, but even video is populated to some degree by people who have no idea what they're doing.

According to one statistic, there are over 450,000 people who earn their living in the audiovisual field in the United States. For all these so-called "specialists" there are a great many who have never received formal training in the business, and still others who have made a career out of it but lack the skills necessary to make it a learning experience for themselves and those around them.

The point is that video, like any other medium, is capable of desensitizing an otherwise receptive audience. If your company is serious about pursuing video on a semi-regular or regular basis, someone is going to have to spell out the company's long-term intentions and stick to them.

This is a good time to ask yourself and others some key questions:

- Will video production require a special division or section to manage and operate?
- If not, will video decisions be centralized? That is, will the same people be involved from project to project? Who will have final approval?
- Is the company willing to create a yearly budget to support video, or will expenses be addressed on a project-by-project basis?
- Are there others who can be assigned to lend production support or share in some of the responsibilities of producing a show?

These and many other questions deserve thorough discussion. You're in the best position to recount everything you had to go through to create your program. The shortcuts and tips you picked up along the way will serve you and the company well. Take your time when discussing the pros and cons and take a hard look at what you can afford and what you can't.

There are no solid guidelines that will help you make these decisions—all companies have their own needs—but there are ways to approach the subject.

The main thing to consider is whether video will be accepted by the people for whom you produce it in the first place. Every executive in the company can give a big thumbs up to a video she considers the best she's ever seen, but if the audience is bored to tears by it, who really benefits?

The people who make up your audience are the best judge of what works and what doesn't. If you want to take their pulse, you need a way to poll them. What you need is a program evaluation.

DESIGNING PROGRAM EVALUATIONS

Instead of rushing in right away to see if your audience is ready to pledge their wholehearted support and undying loyalty to you, wait a bit until the video has had a chance to take hold and sink in. If that process takes several weeks or months, it's worth it. First impressions are important, but for many people video needs to be taken in small doses before it's accepted.

No one likes paperwork, especially if it involves a lot of subjective thought, but a program evaluation can appeal to your viewer on several levels if prepared properly. If well designed and written, an evaluation will reveal far more about your audience than you think.

What Type of Evaluation Will You Need?

There are two basic types of program evaluations: number-based ratings and short essay answers.

Number-based ratings are easy to put together. You ask a series of questions and assign number values to the answers based on positive and negative responses. These are easy to quantify. You add up all the 5s and 10s and assign percentages based on the total number of responses you received.

This type of evaluation doesn't do much to stimulate thought. After watching a program, viewers are handed a sheet of paper with 15 questions on it. Rather than taking time to separate their likes and dislikes, most will simply circle all of the numbers that signify that the program was "good." Not outstanding or horrendous—just "good." This doesn't make for a very accurate reading of the audience's feelings about the subject matter or all the work you put into it.

The other format—short essay answers—can take the form of either checking off an appropriate box or jotting down a concise opinion. You ask a question and leave two or three lines for a response. This format doesn't work particularly well on its own, either, for the same reason as the number-based rating system. Faced with 15 essay questions, the viewer will write "It's good," "No problem with the material," and "Yes."

When you tally up the responses, this is what you'll get: 90% said they thought the program was good, 95% said the presentation was well done, and 100% said they'd like to see more videos. Ego aside, it's not much to work with, is it?

Neither format really provides a thorough means of picking someone's brain. Indeed, relying solely on statistics provides less than satisfying insights.

Forget about the yes-or-no type of program evaluation and concentrate instead on the audience itself. Taking a less direct approach asks questions that might not be anticipated, questions that will tell you quite a bit about the people who are watching your programs. From their responses, you'll receive a clear signal as to whether or not they're buying into your shows.

What Do You Think?

All videos begin with questions. You asked them during your first meeting and you worked through them with the scriptwriter, production company, talent, and editor.

Some of the questions you'll ask in the evaluation are obvious and directly related to the program. Others, as you will see, are less obvious at first, but when analyzed in terms of the whole evaluation, they take on a life all their own.

Sit down and list all the questions you would normally ask if you were to query the audience in person:

- How interesting was the program?
- Was the material clearly presented?
- Was the program easy to understand?
- What did you like best?
- What did you like least?
- How relevant was the material to your life or job?
- Did the program accomplish its objectives? Did you believe in what was said and shown?
- Did the program teach, motivate, or inspire you? In what ways?
- How many times have you seen the video?
- Would you like to see more videos?
- What other subject(s) would you like to see?
- How effective was the program in increasing your awareness of the subject?
- Did the program want to make you learn more about the subject?
- Was the program too long? Too short? Just right?

Now move on to the next level of questioning:

- Job position?
- Job responsibilities?
- What is your length of service with your company?
- Company awards/recognition?
- Training programs completed?
- Professional designations?
- Community involvement?

What do these questions have to do with your video? By asking these questions, you'll find out exactly who your viewers are. You'll get a feel for the kinds of lives they lead, their level of industry expertise, how active they are in continuing education courses and company training programs, and how often they attend company events such as sales meetings and conferences.

Using some of the same methods you used in the treatment, your evaluation should blend all these questions, and others like them, into a format of stops and starts, a format that makes the viewer stop and think a bit about the answers before they're committed to paper.

Figure 17.1 is one suggestion for designing an evaluation. Notice how it balances numbers and essay questions, and how biographical questions hold them together.

EVALUATING RESPONSES

When you receive program responses, the next step is to arrange all of them into some kind of coherent format that managers and executives will understand. In some ways, this is where you make connections between lifestyles, lengths of service, experience, designations, etc., and the success of the program. If you list the responses in a readable order, anyone will be able to understand just how great an impact the program has had on the many levels.

Let's say you receive an overwhelming response to the program. You sit down and read through everyone's answers. Where do you start?

Start with viewer participation. In the following order, break the responses down into:

1. Total number of returned surveys
2. Job position
3. Length of service
4. Company awards/recognition
5. Professional designations
6. Training programs attended

VIDEO SURVEY

Name: (Optional)

Office: (Optional)

Would you please help us assess and improve the effectiveness of video as a company communications tool? We'd appreciate your comments and answers. ALL RESPONSES WILL BE CONFIDENTIAL.

Please indicate which of the following apply to you:

Length of service: 0-1 yr. [ ] 2-5 yrs [ ] 6-10 yrs [ ]

11-15 yrs.[ ] 16-20 yrs[ ] 21+ yrs [ ]

Position:

Job Duties:

Training Programs Attended:

Awards/ Community Recognition:

Professional Designations:

Once you have completed the survey, please return as soon as possible to the home office via mail pouch.

Figure 17.1   Sample Video Survey

VIDEO RATING

Circle the number that most clearly reflects your opinion.

How interesting was the program?

Very Interesting (4)   Reasonably Interesting (3)

Slightly Interesting (2)   Not Interesting (1)

How relevant was the material to your work?

Very Relevant (4)   Reasonably Relevant (3)

Slightly Relevant (2)   Not Relevant (1)

How effective was this program in increasing home office/field communications?

Very Effective (4)   Reasonably Effective (3)

Slightly Effective (2)   Not Effective (1)

How effective was the program in increasing your awareness of the subject?

Very Effective (4)   Reasonably Effective (3)

Slightly Effective (2)   Not Effective (1)

Program length was: Okay [ ]   Too Short [ ]   Too Long [ ]

Additional Comments:

Figure 17.1   Sample Video Survey *(continued)*

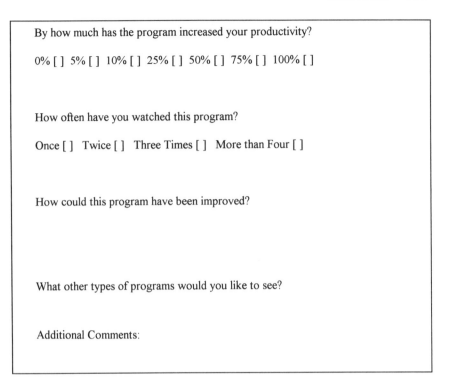

By how much has the program increased your productivity?

0% [ ] 5% [ ] 10% [ ] 25% [ ] 50% [ ] 75% [ ] 100% [ ]

How often have you watched this program?

Once [ ]   Twice [ ]   Three Times [ ]   More than Four [ ]

How could this program have been improved?

What other types of programs would you like to see?

Additional Comments:

Figure 17.1   Sample Video Survey *(continued)*

The result should look something like Figure 17.2.

When someone reads this section, some interesting numbers come into play. Why have people with less than five years' experience sent in more responses? Why haven't more Division Managers participated in the survey? What can you do to reach the 30-year veterans?

You get the idea. The rest of your report can then be broken down into individual responses—by position, designations, etc. Use pie and bar charts. It's up to you.

You won't have much room in your report to list all the short essay responses, so list a dozen or so as they were submitted, both good and bad. A balanced view shows that people are watching the program and that it is generating a wide range of sentiments.

Much as you'd like to bask in the glow of your own genius, keep your perspective. The following is an actual response I received that didn't really single out any one video, but served as an indictment of the whole process:

VIDEO SURVEY REPORT

Program Name: "A Product for All Time"
Program Length: Six Minutes
Total Number of Surveys Sent to Field: 2400
Total Number of Surveys Returned: 1800
Percent Response: 75%

Percent response by position:
Managers--10%
Office Staff--25%
Sales Reps--65%

Response by Length of Service:
0-1 yr--15%
2-5 yrs--50%
6-10 yrs--15%
11-15 yrs--10%
16-20 yrs--8%
21+ yrs--2%

Response by Award/Recognition:
SalesMaster--70%
Community Leadership--25%
Office Best--5%

Professional Designations:
State License ABC--20%
National License DEF--15%

Response by Training Type:
Product Training--55%
Customer Service--20%
Computer Support--25%

Figure 17.2 Video Survey Report

I feel these videos are a waste of time and money. No one is really interested in them, and I don't think they make a bit of difference to anyone's sales production. All we hear about from the home office is how we have to watch our expenses, and then all of a sudden every office was equipped with a monitor, player and stand. Now we're in the video business! This company used to rely on people. Now we're plugged into computers and videos.

I thought the response was honest and passionate. This came from a company veteran who had been through several cutbacks and had made a legitimate point about company priorities. Management didn't take the response all that seriously because it was outnumbered by the positive responses, but I never forgot it.

Take the good with the bad, listen carefully to what people are saying, and strive to take the next program to a higher level of achievement.

WHERE DO YOU GO FROM HERE?

If you should reach a point where you've been assigned to handle all the videos produced by your company, you would do well to standardize your job responsibilities. Figure 17.3 can be used as a way to remind yourself and show others that video production takes a great deal of time and effort to pull off with any measure of success. Have it incorporated into your regular job description.

I've known people who found video production a lot more interesting than what they normally did for their company and asked me if they should look for a new job. However you decide to handle this situation, please don't quit your job after your first show. First of all, the novelty of producing a video for the first time will pass. After a while, planning and producing videos may seem as boring as any other procedure. Second, the video industry is just as susceptible to economic change as any other industry. When companies don't have money to spend, production houses feel the pinch and either cut back on personnel or put all new hiring on hold. Third, without a specialty, getting a job will be difficult. Today's production companies look for people with very specific talents, and competition is fierce.

What's so unusual about the video industry as a whole is that most of the professionals I've worked with never intended to get involved in production. A computer colorist for a major production house played the viola for my high school orchestra. A house producer I worked with was a former dancer. An architect turned into a director. As for myself, I had planned to be an agronomist.

Consider your career options carefully. If you feel you have the drive and talent to be a part of the video industry, start by asking your house producer what opportunities are available. A number of professionals start out as account reps or sales people, gradually working their way up to the role of

TITLE: Video Coordinator/Producer

REPORTS TO: Communications Manager

SUMMARY

At the direction of the Communications Manager this employee will:

1) Research and produce video programs for user departments.

2) Meet with user departments to develop program needs.

3) Manage various stages of program creation and use.

DUTIES

The Video Coordinator/Producer will:

1) Develop proposals for a wide variety of company programs.

2) Research and develop program concepts and content.

3) Meet with department representatives to develop programs.

4) Hire writers, production companies, and other services.

5) Coordinate activities of hired individuals and companies.

6) Attend production meetings, tapings, and editing sessions.

7) Oversee duplication and distribution of programs.

8) Maintain production files and all pertinent video information.

9) Attend video seminars and meetings.

Figure 17.3 Video Job Description

producer. If you already have a talent for art or computer design, offer your services on a freelance basis. Video organizations often post job listings in their newsletters. Let the people you work with know you're interested.

EDUCATE YOURSELF

Your growing files on various aspects of the industry will help keep information at your fingertips. Update this information on a regular basis. If it has been a while since your last show, call to verify union pay schedules for talent or to reconfirm scriptwriter rates. Take every opportunity to learn about new technologies and trends.

In the event that your company creates a separate division for video production and puts you in charge, you should consider taking advantage of the video workshops and classes offered to beginners and professionals alike to improve your skills.

The International Film & Television Workshops of Rockport, Maine, for example, offers more than one hundred courses covering every aspect of video production, from budgeting and planning to basic lighting to directing documentaries. Local video organizations also advertise workshops you can attend. When they are offered, start with basic planning and production classes, then move on to scriptwriting, camera techniques, or whatever else interests you. If your company is serious about its commitment to video, the expense is well worth it.

Effective video programming can be a public relations boon for your company. If you feel like showing other people what you've been up to, there are numerous contests sponsored by local associations to consider. Enter one of your programs. It's a great way for other people to see what you're doing. You might even walk away with an award. You'll definitely become very popular with production houses and other video professionals who would love to help you with the next show. Over time, other companies in your industry will take an interest in your projects and will ask to see some of your shows. If they're thinking about taking the video plunge themselves, you could become their primary contact if they need advice on locating essential services.

What you do with video is up to you. I have spent a great deal of time in this book talking about planning and preparation, but it's difficult to explain it if you haven't experienced it yourself.

Planning is everything. Execution—even when you're talking about creativity—is a natural by-product of all your hard work and dedication. Planning will make or break a program. Not every show will go smoothly, and you'll encounter your share of setbacks and headaches, but it's an experience you'll carry with you for a long time.

Always approach video production with an open mind and a willingness to learn. See how far you can go. And have a good time doing it.

AT THIS STAGE OF THE POST-PRODUCTION
PROCESS YOU SHOULD

- Avoid using video for communications best served by other mediums.
- Understand that video is expendable.
- Design a program evaluation.
- Update any information you receive from production services and vendors.
- Rewrite your job description to cover video production.
- Sign up for video workshops.
- Take every video production for what it is—a chance to expand your personal and professional horizons.

APPENDIX A
Film Commissions

UNITED STATES

Some states, such as Arizona, California, Florida, New York, and Texas, have separate film offices in more than one city or county. Check with your state's commission for local addresses and phone numbers.

Alabama Film Office
401 Adams Avenue, 6th Floor
Montgomery, AL 36104
334/242-4195
800/633-5898
Fax: 334/242-0486

Alaska Film Office
Alaska Department of Commerce
3601 C Street, Suite 700
Anchorage, AK 99503
907/562-4163
Fax: 907/563-3575

Arizona Motion Picture Development Office
3800 N. Central Avenue, Building D
Phoenix, AZ 85012
602/280-1380
800/523-6695
Fax: 602/280-1384

Arkansas Motion Picture Development Office
One Capitol Mall, Suite 2C 200
Little Rock, AR 72201
501/682-7676
Fax: 501/682-FILM

California Film Commission
6922 Hollywood Boulevard, Suite 600
Hollywood, CA 90028
213/736-2465
Fax: 213/736-2522

Colorado Film Commission
1625 Broadway, Suite 1975
Denver, CO 80202
303/572-5444
Fax: 303/572-5099

Connecticut Film Commission
865 Brook Street
Rocky Hill, CT 06067
203/258-4301
Fax: 203/529-0835

Delaware Tourism Office
Delaware Advertising and Media Relations
Box 1401
99 Kings Highway
Dover, DE 19903
302/739-4271
800/441-8846
Fax: 302/739-5749

Mayor's Office of Motion Picture and TV Development
717 14 NW, 10th Floor
Washington, DC 20005
202/727-6600
Fax: 202/727-3787

Florida Film Liaison Office
107 W. Gaines Street
Tallahassee, FL 32399-2000
904/922-5943

Georgia Film and Video Tape Office
Box 1776
Atlanta, GA 30301
404/656-3591
Fax: 404/656-3567

State of Hawaii Film Industry Branch
Department of Business and Economic Development
Grosvenor Center, Mauka Tower
737 Bishop Street, Suite 1900
Honolulu, HI 96813
808/586-2570
Fax: 808/586-2572

Idaho Film Bureau
700 W. State Street
Boise, ID 83720
208/334-2470
800/942-8338
Fax: 208/334-2631

Illinois Film Office
Department of Commerce and Community Affairs
100 W. Randolph Street, Suite 3400
Chicago, IL 60601
312/814-3600
Fax: 312/814-6732

Indiana Film Commission
Indiana Department of Commerce
One N Capitol, Suite 700
Indianapolis, IN 46204-2268
317/232-8829
Fax: 317/232-4146

Iowa Film Office
Iowa Department of Economic Development
200 E. Grand Avenue
Des Moines, IA 50309
515/242-4700
800/779-3456

Kansas Film Commission
Kansas Department of Commerce, Travel, and Tourism Division
700 SW Harrison Street, Suite 1200
Topeka, KS 66603-3712
913/296-4927
Fax: 913/296-6988

Kentucky Film Commission
Kentucky Tourism Cabinet
2200 Capital Plaza Tower
Frankfort, KY 40601
502/564-3456
800/345-6591
Fax: 502/564-7588

Louisiana Film Commission
Box 44320
Baton Rouge, LA 70804-4320
504/342-8150
Fax: 504/342-7988

Maine Film Office
Maine Department of Tourism
State House, Station 59
Augusta, ME 04333
207/287-5705
Fax: 207/287-5701

Maryland Film Commission
601 N. Howard Street
Baltimore, MD 21201
410/333-6633
Fax: 410/333-1062

Massachusetts Office of Film and Video Development
Transportation Building
10 Park Plaza, Suite 2310
Boston, MA 02116
617/973-8800
Fax: 617-973-8810

Michigan Film Office
Department of Commerce
Box 30004
Lansing, MI 48909
517/373-3456
800/477-FILM
Fax: 517/373-3872

Minnesota Film Board
401 N. Third Street, Suite 460
Minneapolis, MN 55401
612/332-6493
Fax: 612/332-3735

Mississippi Film Office
Box 849
Jackson, MS 39205
601/359-3297
Fax: 601/359-2832

Missouri Film Office
Box 1055
Jefferson City, MO 65102
314/751-9050
Fax: 314/751-5160

Montana State Film Office
Montana Travel Promotion Unit
1424 Ninth Avenue
Helena, MT 59620
406/444-2654
800/553-4563
Fax: 406/444-1800

Nebraska Department of Economic Development
Box 94666
301 Centennial Mall S, 4th Floor
Lincoln, NE 68509
402/471-3111
800/426-6505
Fax: 402/471-3778

Nevada Commission on Economic Development
Motion Picture and Television Division
3770 Howard Hughes Parkway, Suite 295
Las Vegas, NV 89158
702/486-7150
Fax: 702/486-7155

New Hampshire Film and TV Bureau
Box 856
Concord, NH 03302-0856
603/271-2598
Fax: 603/271-2629

New Jersey Motion Picture and Television Commission
Box 47023
Newark, NJ 07101
201/648-6279
Fax: 201/648-7350

New Mexico Film Office
1050 Old Pecos Trail
Sante Fe, NM 87501
505/827-7365
800/545-9871
Fax: 505/827-7369

New York State Governor's Office for Motion Picture and TV Development
Pier 62, W 23rd Street, Hudson River, Room 30
New York, NY 10011
212/929-0240
Fax: 212/929-0506

North Carolina Film Office
Department of Commerce
430 N. Salisbury Street
Raleigh, NC 27611
919/733-9900
800/232-9227
Fax: 919/715-0151

North Dakota Film Commission
604 E. Boulevard
Bismarck, ND 58505
701/224-2525
800/435-5663
Fax: 701/224-4878

Ohio Film Commission
Box 1001
77 S. High Street, 29th Floor
Columbus, OH 43266-0101
614/466-2284
800/848-1300
Fax: 614/466-6744

Oklahoma Film Office
440 S. Houston, Suite 4
Tulsa, OK 74127
918/581-2660
800/766-3456
Fax: 918/581-2244

Oregon Film and Video Office
Oregon Economic Development Department
775 Summer NE
Salem, OR 97310
503/373-1232
Fax: 503/581-5115

Pennsylvania Film Bureau
Department of Commerce
449 Forum Building
Harrisburg, PA 17120
717/783-3456
Fax: 717/234-4560

Rhode Island Film Commission
7 Jackson Walkway
Providence, RI 02903
401/277-3456
Fax: 401/277-6046

South Carolina State Film Office
Box 927
Columbia, SC 29202
803/737-0490
Fax: 803/737-0418

South Dakota Film Commission
711 E. Wells Avenue
Pierre, SD 57501-3369
605/773-3301
Fax: 605/773-3256

Tennessee Film, Entertainment, and Music Commission
320 Sixth Avenue N, 7th Floor
Nashville, TN 37243
615/741-3456
800/251-8594
Fax: 615/741-5829

Texas Film Commission
The Office of the Governor
201 E. 14th Street, 3rd Floor
Austin, TX 78701
512/463-9200
Fax: 512/463-4114

Utah Film Commission
324 S. State Street, Suite 500
Salt Lake City, UT 84114-7330
801/538-8740
800/453-8824
Fax: 801/538-8886

Vermont Film Bureau
Agency of Development and Community Affairs
134 State Street
Montpelier, VT 05602
802/828-3236
800/634-8984
Fax: 802/828-3233

Virginia Film Office
State Department of Economic Development
1021 E. Cary Street
Richmond, VA 23219
804/371-8204
Fax: 804/786-1121

Washington State Film and Video Office
Department of Trade and Economic Development
2001 6th Avenue, Suite 2700
Seattle, WA 98121
206/464-7148
Fax: 206/464-5868

West Virginia Film Office
2101 Washington Street E
Charleston, WV 25305
304/558-2286
800/CALL-WVA
Fax: 304/558-0108

Wisconsin Film Office
Box 7970
123 W. Washington Avenue
Madison, WI 53707
608/267-FILM
Fax: 608/266-3403

Wyoming Film Office
Interstate 25 and College Drive
Cheyenne, WY 82002
307/777-7777
800/458-6657
Fax: 307/777-6904

Puerto Rican Film Commission Industries
Fonento Building
335 FD Roosevelt Avenue, Suite 107
Hato Rey, PR 00918
809/758-4747
Fax: 809/756-5706

Virgin Islands Film Promotion Office
Department of Economic Development and Agriculture
Box 6400
St. Thomas, VI 00804
809/775-1444
Fax: 809/774-4390

CANADA

Alberta Film Commissioner's Office
Economic Development Sterling Place
9940 106 Street, 10th Floor
Edmonton, AB T5K 2P6, Canada
403/427-2005
Fax: 403/427-5924

British Columbia Film Commission
601 W. Cordova Street
Vancouver, BC V6B 1G1, Canada
604/660-2732
Fax: 604/660-4790

CIDO-Location Manitoba
93 Lombard Avenue, Suite 333
Winnipeg, MB R3B 3B1, Canada
204/947-2040
Fax: 204/956-5261

New Brunswick Film and Video Commission
Box 6000
Fredericton, NB E3B 5H1, Canada
506/453-2553
Fax: 506/453-2416

Nova Scotia Film Development Corporation
1724 Granville Street
Halifax, NS B3J 1X5, Canada
902/424-7185
Fax: 902/424-0563

Ontario Film Development Corporation
175 Bloor Street E, N Tower, Suite 300
Toronto, ON M4W 3R8, Canada
416/314-6858
Fax: 416/314-6876

Montreal Film Commission-CIDEC Cinema
500 Rene/Levesque Boulevard
Montreal, PQ H2L 4Y3, Canada
514/872-2883
Fax: 514/872-1153

SASKFILM
1840 McIntrye Street, 2nd Floor
Regina, SK S4P 2P9, Canada
306/347-3456
Fax: 306/359-7768

Yukon Film Promotion Office
Box 2703
Whitehorse, YT Y1A 2C6, Canada
403/667-5400
Fax: 403/667-2634

APPENDIX B

Video Publications

Audio-Visual Communications
PTN Publishing Co.
445 Broad Hollow Road, Suite 21
Melville, NY 11747
516/845-2700
Fax: 516/845-7109

AV Video
Montage Publishing Inc.
701 Westchester Avenue, Suite 109W
White Plains, NY 10604
914/328-9157
Fax: 914/328-9093

The Professional Communicator
Women in Communications, Inc.
3717 Columbia Pike, Suite 310
Arlington, VA 22204
703/920-5555
Fax: 703/920-5556

Video Systems
Intertec Publishing Corp.
Box 12901
9800 Metcalf
Overland Park, KS 66212
913/341-1300
Fax: 913/967-1898

Videography
PSN Publications
2 Park Ave., Suite 1820
New York, NY 10016
212/779-1919
Fax: 212/213-3484

Videomaker Magazine
Box 4591
Chico, CA 95927
916/891-8410
Fax: 916/891-8443

Visual Media
Ontario Film Association, Inc.
2053 Rebecca Street
Oakville, ON L6L 2A1, Canada
416/575-2076

APPENDIX C
Video Organizations and Associations

American Film and Video Association
Sound and Moving Image Library, York University
4700 Keele Street
North York, ON M3J 1P3, Canada
416/736-5508
Fax: 416/736-5830

American Women in Radio and Television, Inc.
1101 Connecticut Avenue NW, Suite 700
Washington, DC 20036
202/429-5102
Fax: 202/223-4579

Association for Multi-Image International, Inc. (AMI)
10008 N. Dale Mabry Highway, Suite 113
Tampa, FL 33618
813/960-1692
Fax: 813/962-7911

Association of Visual Communicators (AVC)
8130 La Mesa Boulevard, Suite 406
La Mesa, CA 92194-6437
619/461-1600
Fax: 619/461-1606

Audio Visual Management Association (AVMA)
607 Arbor Avenue
Wheaton, IL 60189
708/653-2772
Fax: 708/653-2882

215

International Television Association (ITVA)
6311 N. O'Connor Road, Suite 230
Irving, TX 75039
214/869-1112
Fax: 214/869-2980

University Film and Video Association (UFVA)
7101 W. 80th Street
Los Angeles, CA 90045
310/338-3033
Fax: 310/338-3030

Women In Communications Inc.
3717 Columbia Pike, Suite 310
Arlington, VA 22204
703/920-5555
Fax: 703/920-5556

APPENDIX D

Video Book Publishers

Audio Video Market Place
R.R. Bowker Company
121 Chanlon Road
New Providence, NJ 07974
908/665-6719
800/521-8110
A directory of over 7,000 manufacturers, services, periodicals, festivals, reference books, manufacturers, distributors, and production services in the United States and Canada.

Educational Technology Publications, Inc.
700 Palisade Avenue
Englewood Cliffs, NJ 07632
201/871-4007
Fax: 201/871-4009

Focal Press
313 Washington Street
Newton, MA 02158
617/928-2500

Knowledge Industry Publications, Inc.
701 Westchester Avenue
White Plains, NY 10604
914/328-9157
Fax: 914/328-9093

Oryx Press
4041 N. Central Avenue, Suite 700
Phoenix, AZ 85012-3397
602/265-2651
Fax: 602/265-6250

Prentice-Hall Inc.
Route 9W
Englewood Cliffs, NJ 07632
201/592-2000
Fax: 201/592-0696

TAB Books/McGraw Hill, Inc.
Box 40, Monterey Avenue
Blue Ridge Summit, PA 17294-0850
717/794-2191
Fax: 717/794-2080

Wadsworth Publishing Company
10 Davis Drive
Belmont, CA 94002
415/595-2350
Fax: 606/625-0978

APPENDIX E

Scriptwriting Software

The following software programs are not recommended, but are merely provided for your information. Any good word processor can be formatted to handle scripts, but these programs are designed specifically for today's writer.

FULL-FEATURED PROGRAMS

ScriptMaster
Comprehensive Video Supply Corporation
148 Veterans Drive
Northvale, NJ 07647
800/526-0242
Fax: 201/767-7377

Automates the scriptwriting process through menus that allow you to work with up to four columns and a wide field for standard word processing. Includes a spell checker and sophisticated print formats.

IXION Split/Scripter
Ixion, Incorporated
1335 N. Northlake Way
Seattle, WA 98103
206/547-8801
Fax: 206/547-8802

Unlike ScriptMaster, the Ixion Split/Scripter allows you to work only in two-column mode, but it does allow you to insert storyboard boxes, works easily with most printers, and has sophisticated text manipulation features.

WORD PROCESSING ENHANCERS

AVScripter
Tom Schroeppel
4705 Bay View Avenue
Tampa, FL 33611
Using a word processor, codes are inserted before the start of each paragraph type; that is, a ".V" if you want something on the video side, and ".A" for the audio side. After you save the file in an ASCII format, it is read through AVScripter and automatically formatted into a two-column format.

ShowScape
Lake Compuframes, Inc.
P.O. Box 890
Briarcliff Manor, NY 10510
914/941-1998
Fax: 914/941-2043
Uses a variety of word processors, both IBM-based and Macintosh, to create both 2-column and screenplay formats.

WORD PROCESSING ADD-ONS

SuperScript
Inherit the Earth Technologies
1800 S. Robertson Blvd. Suite 326
Los Angeles, CA 90035
213/559-3814
Uses WordPerfect macros to formats scripts into a screenplay style.

SHAREWARE

Some public access programs, found on electronic services such as CompuServe, offer scriptwriting programs that use a word processor's macro capabilities. Check with individual forums for more information. Be very careful, however, because computer viruses are easily transmitted through public access software.

Index

Installation Instructions for The Producer's Assistant

IN A WINDOWS ENVIRONMENT

1. Insert disk into drive A.
2. Double click on your MAIN icon.
3. Double click on FILE MANAGER.
4. Double click on the A drive icon.
5. In the list of files on the A drive, double click on SETUP.EXE.
6. Follow the instructions that appear on screen and the software will be installed.
7. In order to run the ARCHIVE function you will have to copy and edit your AUTOEXEC.BAT. To do this, exit to DOS and key the following series of commands. Please note that commands that come before the "greater than" symbol (>) are the commands you will automatically see on your computer screen. Commands that come after the "greater than" symbol (>) are commands that you should key in. These commands will be in **UPPERCASE BOLD LETTERS**. Keyboard spaces (spacebar) will be represented by _ , and the return key will be represented by **[enter]**.

   C:\WINDOWS>**CD_..[enter]**

   C:\>**COPY_AUTOEXEC.BAT_AUTOEXEC.OLD[enter]**

   C:\>**EDIT_AUTOEXEC.BAT[enter]**

8. Move your cursor down to the second line of the program that begins with SET. Then **[enter]**
9. Move your cursor up to the blank line and key in:

   SET_CLIPPER=F23

10. With your mouse, drag down the FILE menu and SAVE, then EXIT.
11. This will return you to DOS.

    C:\>**EXIT[enter]**

12. This will return you to Windows.
13. To print out the User Documentation, open the file TPADOC.ASC in your word processor and print.

IN A DOS ENVIRONMENT

1. Insert disk into drive A.
2. A series of commands is required to install this program under DOS. Please note that commands that come before the "greater than" symbol (>) are the commands you will automatically see on your computer screen. Commands that come after the "greater than" symbol (>) are commands that you should key in. These commands will be in **UPPERCASE BOLD LETTERS**. Keyboard spaces (spacebar) will be represented by _ , and the return key will be represented by **[enter]**.

   C:\>**A: [enter]**

   A:\>**INSTALL[enter]**

   C:\TPA>**CD_..[enter]**

   C:\>**COPY_AUTOEXEC.BAT_AUTOEXEC.OLD[enter]**

   C:\>**EDIT_AUTOEXEC.BAT[enter]**

3. Move your cursor down to the second line of the program that begins with SET. Then

   [enter]

4. Move your cursor up to the blank line and key:

   SET_CLIPPER=F23

5. Press the ALT key and the (letter) F key at the same time.
6. Press the (letter) S key.
7. Press the ALT key and the (letter) F key at the same time.
8. Press the (letter) X key.

9. This will return you to DOS. Key in the following commands to print out the User Reference Manual.

   C:\>**CD TPA[enter]**

   C:\TPA>**PRINT_TPADOC.ASC**

10. DOS may prompt you for the "Name of list device [PRN]:" You don't have to key anything in, just press **[enter]**.
11. You are now ready to enter the program.

   C:\TPA>**TPA[enter]**